LOUISE FARRENC: NONET FOR WINDS AND STRINGS

As well as being a virtuoso pianist, Louise Farrenc became the first woman to hold a permanent position as professor at the Paris Conservatoire while continuing to compose symphonic and chamber music. This handbook introduces readers to Farrenc and her contemporaries with a focus on professional women musicians in nineteenth-century Paris. Farrenc's music was much admired by her contemporaries, including Robert Schumann and Hector Berlioz. The acclaimed Nonet (1849) incorporated playful dialogue within the ensemble, virtuosic display, and an artful balance of newer and older compositional methods, garnering critical and artistic success and official recognition for the composer. Its performance history shows how musicians managed the logistics of professional life: forming and sustaining relationships, organizing concerts and tours, and promoting their work in the musical press. The book's nuanced analytical approach and historical insights will allow students, performers, and listeners a fresh appreciation of Farrenc's work.

MARIE SUMNER LOTT is an Associate Professor in the School of Music at Georgia State University. She is the author of *The Social Worlds of Nineteenth-Century Chamber Music* (2015), which was awarded the AMS 75 PAYS publication subvention from the American Musicological Society, and over a dozen articles and book chapters on nineteenth-century chamber music.

LOUISE FARRENC: NONET FOR WINDS AND STRINGS

MARIE SUMNER LOTT
Georgia State University

CAMBRIDGE
UNIVERSITY PRESS

Shaftesbury Road, Cambridge CB2 8EA, United Kingdom

One Liberty Plaza, 20th Floor, New York, NY 10006, USA

477 Williamstown Road, Port Melbourne, VIC 3207, Australia

314–321, 3rd Floor, Plot 3, Splendor Forum, Jasola District Centre,
New Delhi – 110025, India

103 Penang Road, #05–06/07, Visioncrest Commercial, Singapore 238467

Cambridge University Press is part of Cambridge University Press & Assessment,
a department of the University of Cambridge.

We share the University's mission to contribute to society through the pursuit of
education, learning and research at the highest international levels of excellence.

www.cambridge.org
Information on this title: www.cambridge.org/9781009415453

DOI: 10.1017/9781009415446

First published 2025

A catalogue record for this publication is available from the British Library

Library of Congress Cataloging-in-Publication Data
NAMES: Sumner Lott, Marie, author.
TITLE: Louise Farrenc : Nonet for winds and strings / Marie Sumner Lott.
DESCRIPTION: [1.] | Cambridge, United Kingdom ; New York : Cambridge University Press, 2025.
| Series: New Cambridge music handbooks | Includes bibliographical references and index.
IDENTIFIERS: LCCN 2025011444 | ISBN 9781009415453 (hardback) | ISBN 9781009415477
(paperback) | ISBN 9781009415446 (ebook)
SUBJECTS: LCSH: Farrenc, Louise, 1804–1875. Nonet, flute, oboe, clarinet, bassoon, horn, violin,
viola, cello, double bass, op. 38, E♭ major. | Farrenc, Louise, 1804–1875 – Criticism and
interpretation. | Music – 19th century – History and criticism.
CLASSIFICATION: LCC ML410.F227 S86 2025 | DDC 780.92–dc23/eng/20250317
LC record available at https://lccn.loc.gov/2025011444

ISBN 978-1-009-41545-3 Hardback
ISBN 978-1-009-41547-7 Paperback

CONTENTS

List of Figures   *page* vi
List of Tables   vii
List of Musical Examples   viii

Introduction to the Life and Career of Louise Farrenc   1
   The Virtuoso Pianist-Composer of the 1820s–1830s   5
   The Composer of "Serious" Music, 1840s to 1860   14

1 Cultivating an Audience for Chamber Music
   in 1840s Paris   23
   Promoting Chamber Music in Early Nineteenth-Century Paris   29
   Thérèse Wartel and the "Cult of Classical and Severe Music"   32
   The Society for Classical Music   42

2 Dialogue and Play in the Nonet   58
   Understanding Form in Nineteenth-Century Music   60
   Movement 1: Adagio – Allegro   66
   Movement 2: Andante con moto   81
   Movement 3: Scherzo Vivace   93
   Movement 4: Adagio – Allegro   99

3 Reception and Legacy of Farrenc's Nonet   118
   The Nonet Leads to Wider Recognition of Farrenc's
   Accomplishments   122
   The Prix Chartier   127
   The Posthumous Legacy of Farrenc and Her Nonet   130

Bibliography   143
Index   149

FIGURES

2.1 Visual aid showing the different parts of the *page* 61
"grande coupe binaire" (sonata form) from
Anton Reicha, *Treatise on Musical
Composition* (1826), p. 300.
2.2 English translation of Reicha's visual aid. 62

TABLES

1.1   List of works performed by the Society for   *page* 45
Classical Music.

2.1   Overview of sonata form in Farrenc Nonet,   68
movement 1 (Allegro).

2.2   Overview of variations form in Farrenc Nonet,   85
movement 2 (Andante).

2.3   Overview of ternary form in Farrenc Nonet,   94
movement 3 (Scherzo vivace).

2.4   Overview of sonata form in Farrenc Nonet,   101
movement 4 (Allegro).

MUSICAL EXAMPLES

2.1   Farrenc Nonet, movement 1, mm. 24–45   *page* 70
      (first mother idea).
2.2   Farrenc Nonet, movement 1, mm. 107–120   73
      ("purple patch" in exposition).
2.3   Farrenc Nonet, movement 1, mm. 160–192   75
      (exposition second ending and new development
      theme).
2.4   Farrenc Nonet, movement 1, mm. 381–391   80
      (violin cadenza and beginning of Coda).
2.5a Beethoven Septet, movement 4, mm. 1–16   83
      (main theme).
2.5b Farrenc Nonet, movement 2, mm. 1–16   84
      (main theme).
2.6a Beethoven Septet, movement 4, mm. 81–88   88
      (Variation 4, first half).
2.6b Farrenc Nonet, movement 2, mm. 65–73   89
      (Variation 4, first half).
2.7   Hummel Septet, movement 3, mm. 112–128   91
      (Variation 3).
2.8   Farrenc Nonet, movement 3, mm. 1–24   96
      (Scherzo main theme).
2.9   Farrenc Nonet, movement 3, mm. 47–64   97
      ("Hunt" theme).
2.10 Farrenc Nonet, movement 4, mm. 37–54   103
      (contrapuntal bridge or second mother idea).
2.11 Farrenc Nonet, movement 4, mm. 94–123   105
      (fugue in the development section).
2.12 Farrenc Nonet, movement 4, mm. 176–216   109
      (new transition material in the recapitulation
      and second mother idea rescored).

INTRODUCTION TO THE LIFE AND CAREER
OF LOUISE FARRENC

The Nonet in E flat for winds and strings, Op. 38 (1849), is an unusual work in Louise Farrenc's output. It is her only surviving chamber work without piano – her three symphonies and two concert overtures are the only other pieces in her catalog of forty-nine numbered works that do not use the piano – and it was composed for a nonstandard ensemble that combines the woodwind quintet (flute, oboe, clarinet, bassoon, and horn) with four orchestral string instruments (violin, viola, violoncello, and double bass) to create a large chamber ensemble of virtuoso soloists. Unlike the piano trio, string quartet, or even the Parisian salon quintet with double bass,[1] ensemble types that had generated dozens of works since the end of the eighteenth century, to the point that phrases like "piano trio" or "string quartet" indicated not just the ensemble of instruments or players, but a musical genre itself with specific compositional conventions and expectations, the nonet as such was new in the nineteenth century. Although it echoes earlier genres like the divertimento and serenade for winds or for winds and strings, or the "Harmoniemusik" of eighteenth-century aristocratic courts, Farrenc's Nonet belongs to an emergent nineteenth-century concert tradition of large chamber ensembles that had become popular in Paris at the beginning of the century. Septets, octets, and even diecettos (for ten instruments) with and without piano had become important centerpieces for some chamber-music concerts, where they provided a theatrical "hook" for audiences who wanted something that stood apart from the standard trios and quartets on offer at most such events. This specific instrumentation had only two precedents before Farrenc composed her work: the Nonet in F major, Op. 31, composed in 1813 by violinist Louis Spohr (1784–1859) at the request of his Viennese patron Johann von Tost, and the Nonet in A minor, Op. 77, by Farrenc's contemporary George Onslow

(1784–1853), which he composed for performance by Paris's Society for Classical Music in 1848.

Farrenc (1804–1875) was at the height of her career as a composer in 1849, riding a wave of critical and public acclaim for her symphonies and chamber music, as well as her solo piano compositions. Celebrated as a "learned" musician and composer of "serious" music, she had earned a reputation over the previous decade as one of Paris's best composers of the *juste milieu*, or the "middle way" between the old and the new styles. How and why did her specific situation, and that of Paris's chamber concert scene, lead her to write an esoteric work for wind instruments instead of, for example, a set of string quartets or a piano quartet at this juncture? How did this unusual piece capture the tastes and idiosyncrasies of Parisian audiences at this historical moment, leading it to be her most renowned work, destined to be performed and praised throughout her lifetime despite the challenges it posed (and still poses) to performers and concert organizers?

This handbook invites readers to enter into Farrenc's musical world in order to explore the Nonet as a work that is simultaneously extraordinary, on the one hand, not only for its craftsmanship and its expressive potency but also by virtue of its unusual instrumentation, while on the other hand being wholly representative of the day-to-day musical culture of mid-nineteenth-century Paris. Chapter 1 begins by setting the scene with a description of Farrenc's grand solo concert on March 19, 1850, when the Nonet was publicly premiered, so that readers less familiar with the concert conventions and culture of the period will have some sense of what it might have been like to hear this work in the original setting for which it was created. The chapter then recounts the series of events that led up to that performance and made possible the composition and presentation of the Nonet. Throughout the 1840s, Farrenc worked within a network of like-minded musicians (including performers, salonnières, and composers) to expand Parisian interest in instrumental music, especially in genres associated at the time with German composers and with "serious" compositional styles. Histories of music in Paris have tended to focus on musical theater, especially French and Italian opera, and on the culture surrounding virtuoso performers, with some discussion of developments in orchestral writing (focused, often, on Hector Berlioz's innovations) and instrument design. These professional activities generally took place in public venues and were often written about in music journals and newspapers, making them "visible" to modern scholars. Chamber music, however, occurred primarily at home and in the semi-private, semi-public space of the salon or the "house concert." A great part of its appeal was the intimate setting and feeling of being included in an event designed for a select few listeners. That setting also meant that it was the special purview of women musicians, who could participate without the stigma associated at that time with putting themselves on public display. During the middle decades of the nineteenth century, Louise Farrenc and the circle of professional and semi-professional women performers, composers, and teachers to which she belonged sustained public interest in a growing canon of earlier chamber works from the eighteenth century, and they created or inspired new works that developed that style further. The role that women musicians played in creating an audience for "serious" chamber music in Paris at and after the middle of the century has not yet been fully acknowledged in music history. Even more surprising for modern readers, perhaps, is the role that music for winds played in bringing audiences to these concerts and making these events memorable for critics, thereby preserving them for modern musicians and historians.

Chapter 2, the heart of the book, takes readers through the Nonet movement-by-movement to show how Farrenc used her intimate knowledge of Parisian tastes and her familiarity with the repertoire and conventions of Classical and Romantic music to negotiate changing expectations of listeners and musicians at the mid-century. The Nonet and Farrenc's other chamber works created a bridge between musical traditions that would make possible later innovations in instrumental music by the likes of Gabriel Fauré and César Franck. The analysis in Chapter 2 highlights the playful interactions and dialogue that make the Nonet engaging for performers and listeners, as well as Farrenc's innovative approach to form and structure that mark the Nonet as a consummate work of compositional craft and ingenuity. Chapter 3 concludes the

Handbook with a discussion of the Nonet's reception and legacy by exploring the ways in which it and Farrenc's other chamber works formed a foundation for critical acclaim in the composer's lifetime but were ultimately forgotten by later generations who were all too happy to push aside composers of the middle decades, characterized as too beholden to a German or Viennese classical past, in their rush to support a nascent French nationalist tradition in the last quarter of the century.

Before turning to the Nonet, though, we should consider how Louise Farrenc came to be one of the most celebrated pianist-composers of mid-century Paris and the roles that Paris's early nineteenth-century musical culture, its institutions, and the people associated with them played in her development as an artist and musician. The discussion that follows draws upon earlier scholarship by Bea Friedland, Catherine Legras, and Christin Heitmann, while also offering for the first time English translations of important reviews and responses to Farrenc and her music published during and after her lifetime as well as new analysis of these in the context of Paris's complex musical culture.[2] However, the available record of Farrenc's life remains frustratingly incomplete and scattered at the time of this writing, as Heitmann noted twenty years ago in her book on Farrenc's chamber and orchestral music.[3] Bea Friedland's 1980 book (based on her 1975 dissertation) remains the best biographical source and the only one in English, but it contains errors and omissions awaiting correction. Louise Farrenc's (documented) surviving correspondence includes just eighteen letters in the Bibliothèque nationale de France, but Heitmann also cites twelve letters preserved in various German and Austrian archives. None of these are currently available to the public online or in published/translated editions (and they are not provided in full in either Friedland's or Heitmann's book). Revelations like these indicate that a more thorough search for sources among Aristide and Louise Farrenc's known contacts is still needed in order to get a complete picture of the couple's life and work. In the meantime, the information we do have about Louise Farrenc and her career entices us to learn as much as we can about this fascinating composer.

The Virtuoso Pianist-Composer of the 1820s–1830s

Born in 1804 into a family of artists employed by the French crown, or the French government during France's Republican years, Jeanne-Louise Dumont grew up in an artistic community housed together in apartments owned by the state nearby to the Sorbonne. She initially studied piano with a family friend, and when she showed a precocious talent for solfège and composition in addition to performance, she was allowed to study privately with composer Anton Reicha, who was employed as a professor of counterpoint and harmony at the Paris Conservatoire du Musique, or Conservatory. Her family's devotion to art and craftsmanship alongside its relatively secure middle-class status meant that Jeanne-Louise had opportunities and support to pursue her craft professionally, unlike women born into more elevated social strata, such as Fanny Mendelssohn, or women born into lower status without the financial resources or time to pursue further studies. Because Jeanne-Louise was the younger of just two children and her parents were securely middle-class, she likely had few if any household duties and did not need to earn an income as a child laborer, maid, or governess to help support her family. In this way, we could say that she grew up in a sort of social "sweet spot" for artistic development. At the same time, her parents seem to have had no expectation that she would take up the life of a touring virtuoso, as many young musicians (men and women) did in the early nineteenth century, often with prompting from teachers and/or family members who sought to capitalize on their status as prodigies (such as Clara Wieck Schumann and, to a lesser extent, Carl Maria von Weber). Rather, Louise studied with local teachers and took full advantage of Paris's thriving music culture to gain further knowledge of contemporaneous musical tastes and traditions. According to a biographical sketch published in 1866, she consulted with pianists Ignaz Moscheles and Johann Nepomuk Hummel about her technique as a young woman, but there's no evidence to suggest that she studied formally with either of them.[4] (Both artists spent significant time in Paris during the 1820s, and Hummel became a family friend and professional colleague;

Louise's husband Aristide Farrenc published many of Hummel's compositions in the 1830s.)

Jeanne-Louise's early years coincided with the "Napoleonic" wars that eventually engulfed the entire European continent and spilled into colonial holdings and disputed territories in North Africa, the Middle East, and North America. Despite the turmoil occurring on the larger world stage, the situation in Paris was relatively secure, in part because the city and its artistic institutions served Bonaparte's mission to project imperial authority and the efficiency of centralized power in the capital. Indeed, the Napoleonic years offered Paris's middle and upper classes a renewed sense of stability and luxury after the violence of the Revolution and its aftermath, and this led to increased opportunities for local musicians. The first decades of the century saw a return of opulent church music, which had been banned during the revolutionary era, and grand theatrical productions that celebrated a triumphant national French identity and revolutionary valor.[5] After Napoleon's abdication and final defeat in 1815, the Bourbon Restoration brought émigrés back to France; many musicians who had fled to cities like London or Vienna returned to Paris, where they now founded schools, factories for instrument making, publishing houses, and concert series. The music industry flourished in Paris during the 1820s, driven in part by the "Rossini craze" that generated a wave of new compositions, arrangements, parodies, and souvenir editions of excerpts from the Italian operas being performed at the Théâtre-Italien and at other theaters throughout Paris's suburbs. Rossini himself spent the years 1824–1829 in the capital, where he not only led new performances of Italian favorites but also created French versions of his recent works and composed new operas specifically for the French stage, such as the opéra comique *Le Comte Ory* in 1828 and *Guillaume Tell* in 1829. He brought Giacomo Meyerbeer to Paris in 1824 to stage that composer's heroic opera *Il Crociato in Egitto*. During the 1830s, Rossini, Meyerbeer, and Daniel Auber developed a new operatic style ("French Grand Opera") that would have a far-reaching impact throughout Europe and North America for the next several decades.

6

Jeanne-Louise developed her musical instincts and compositional skill in this climate of sumptuousness, in which lavish opera productions coexisted with simpler sentimental romances by popular composers like Loïsa Puget (1810–1889) and August Panseron (1796–1859), and an expanding culture of virtuoso salon and concert performances brought these two modes of expression together for an adoring public. Her early compositions show her to be an inventive creator of popular virtuoso works, well versed in the dominant piano styles and genres of her day, but not a slavish imitator of others. In 1821, when she was seventeen years old, Jeanne-Louise married the flutist, composer, and publisher Aristide Farrenc (1794–1865), who would prove to be a supportive partner and collaborator on musical projects. Aristide encouraged his wife to continue her studies with Reicha, to publish her compositions (her early works were published by his firm), and to perform publicly. Louise Farrenc, as she would be known from then on, published one of her own compositions for the first time in 1822, when Aristide's firm issued her *Variations brillantes* on a theme by Aristide, Op. 2. By 1825, she had published a series of quadrilles – a social dance popular in the parlors and salons of Europe in the first half of the nineteenth century – based on melodies from popular operas of the early 1820s. (Aristide Farrenc's firm published them without opus numbers in 1825; they paraphrased melodies from C. M. von Weber's *Der Freischütz*, Mozart's *Entführung aus dem Serail*, and Meyerbeer's *Il Crociato in Egitto*. Around 1830 she also published a set of quadrilles on national airs.[6]) In the next fifteen years, she would compose and publish over twenty solo piano works in the virtuoso style, mostly sets of variations and rondos. About half of these were based on popular opera melodies being heard in Paris's theaters and salons at the time, including Rossini's *La Cenerentola* and *Zelmire*; Bellini's *Il Pirata*, *I Capuleti e I Montecchi*, and *Norma*; Donizetti's *Anna Bolena*; George Onslow's *Le Colporteur*; Weber's *Euryanthe*; and Meyerbeer's *Les Huguenots*. The majority of Farrenc's piano compositions in these years were issued in simultaneous editions by Aristide's firm in Paris and by various international publishers: J. Duff in London, Peters in Leipzig, Simrock in Bonn,

Aible in Munich, and Böhme in Hamburg. In this decade, Farrenc also made arrangements of popular works by pianists Henri Herz and Franz Hünten, primarily for German publishers. These arrangements gave her further insight into the virtuoso techniques of her day, which she would then use in her own compositions, in addition to building her reputation with publishers and audiences. Her original compositions published in the 1830s often bore dedications to important patrons and performers in Farrenc's growing network of French musicians; the majority of these honor other women, mostly pianists. Farrenc dedicated two works to the salon hostess and piano teacher Sophie Pierson-Bodin (1819–1874), who was her only dedicatee to receive multiple dedications: the *Variations sur une galopade favorite hongroise*, Op. 12 (1833) and the *Trente Études dans tous les tons majeurs et mineurs*, Op. 26 (1839). Farrenc also dedicated her *Variations brillantes sur la cavatine d'Anna Bolena de Donizetti*, op. 15 (1835) to the composer and pianist Leopoldine Blahetka (1809–1885), a child prodigy who had established a virtuoso career in Vienna, then gave several tours throughout Europe in the next two decades; she and her family moved to France in 1830. Farrenc's dedications of her published works to fellow professional women musicians like these, as opposed to wealthy amateurs, helped her to build and sustain a network of professional women in Paris and its environs. That ever-expanding network would support and sustain her throughout her career, and she would use it to lift up other young women, including her pupils, over the next several decades.

The first mention in the press of Louise Farrenc as a performer comes from January 1828, when she and Aristide played in a soirée hosted by the piano manufacturer Jean-Henri Pape. Throughout the nineteenth century, it was common for instrument builders to host concert series in specially built recital halls or large salons at their homes or factories. These allowed them to build and maintain collaborative relationships with artists who would purchase and promote their instruments and to demonstrate the latest developments in instrument design and manufacture. Demonstrating the reciprocal relationship between builders and players of instruments, reviews of major concerts in these years frequently mention the

8

piano builder who provided instruments for the evening's performance and praised new features that enhanced the sound. During her lifetime, Farrenc and her students would play at the Salle Pleyel, the Salle Érard, and the Salle Saxe, in addition to private salons and larger theaters. The program at Pape's soirée opened with a *Fantaisie* for flute and piano "composed and executed by Monsieur and Madame Farrenc," and Louise performed with Hieronymus (Jérome) Payer a set of variations for two pianos (composed by Payer) in the concert's second half.[7]

Two years later, in July 1830, the Farrencs gave a major concert featuring works by their friend Johann Nepomuk Hummel (1778–1837), who also played an improvisation at the end of the concert. The announcement and subsequent review in the *Revue musicale* described the event as a concert "given by Mme Farrenc," probably because she appeared on the program as featured pianist in the ensemble work that opened the concert and as piano soloist later in the evening.[8] The recurring columns "News from Paris" and "News from the departments" were typically unsigned, but the reviewer was probably François-Joseph Fétis (1784–1871), who had founded the *Revue musicale* in 1827. Fétis served as both editor and head critic for the journal, and he wrote lead articles for it that presented his original research into the history of music and the science of sound. (In 1835. the *Revue musicale* merged with a musical newspaper published by Maurice Schlesinger, and the resulting *Revue et Gazette musicale de Paris* became one of the most important journals devoted to concert music in France until it ceased publication in 1880.) Fétis was a friend and colleague of Aristide Farrenc, who would work with him on musicological studies and historical concerts until Aristide's death in 1865.[9] Fétis championed Louise Farrenc's orchestral compositions in Brussels after he moved to that city in 1833 to become director of the Royal Conservatory of Brussels.

The July 1830 review described Louise Farrenc's performance using language that would become common in discussions of her and her works over the next decade:

This young lady, who through serious studies acquired on the piano a very distinguished talent, was able to resist the frivolous taste which has made this instrument a mechanical one, where only the agility of the fingers is noticed, and the genius of the artist is not taken into account. She has followed [instead] the road traced by Hummel, Moscheles, Kalkbrenner and seems destined to obtain honorable successes there. She was justly applauded in an unpublished military septet by Hummel [Op. 114 published in 1831], as well as in a rondo and in an adagio by this master.[10]

The association of Farrenc and her music with "serious study" and with an apparent refusal to succumb to mere "frivolity" and "mechanical" virtuosic display would become an important aspect of her public persona. As with other women pianists of her generation, critics valued Farrenc's adherence to a classical ideal of restraint and balance in her programming and performance, noting that she played with greater understanding and depth than lesser (usually unnamed) contemporaries.[11] Significantly, the Hummel Military Septet that was premiered on this concert is a mixed large-ensemble work for piano, flute, clarinet, trumpet, violin, violoncello, and double bass. Because it was a newly composed work by a popular and well-respected composer and because of its unusual and characteristic instrumentation – the interplay of trumpet and other winds suggested military bands for contemporaneous listeners, and Hummel used them to good effect with fanfares and other martial topics that capitalized on this association – the work made a strong impression on listeners and critics. Throughout the first half of the nineteenth century, chamber music concerts included works like this, at least in part, to capture the attention of Parisian audiences through novelty and variety of timbres. That the Farrencs recognized this useful aspect of wind chamber music already in their 1830 debut concert points forward to Louise's engagement with wind players later in her career up to and beyond the creation of her Nonet.

A few days after Louise Farrenc's successful 1830 concert, Parisians took to the streets to protest the July Ordinances, a set of restrictive laws enacted by Charles X's government in an attempt to hold onto power despite increased opposition to its conservative policies from progressive representatives in the Parliament. The July Revolution, also known as the "Three Glorious Days," established a new constitutional monarchy in France. The crown moved from the Bourbon family to the house of Orléans, and the provisional government adopted a new charter that further limited the monarch's powers and concentrated voting and governing rights within the ranks of the landed gentry and rich bourgeoisie. The July Monarchy oversaw a rapid industrialization in France in the 1830s and 1840s, including the expansion of railway systems and factory networks that began to concentrate the population in cities and larger towns. For the upper middle classes, to which Aristide and Louise Farrenc belonged, these were good years, as the new king Louis Philippe and his cabinet instituted policies and government subsidies that were favorable to business and supported a growing bourgeoisie. Paris became the "capital of Europe," with musicians flocking to the city to study at the Conservatory, to perform at the many opera houses and theaters (or to have their compositions performed there), and to give concerts. The violin virtuoso Niccolò Paganini conquered Paris in 1831, and his performances there and throughout Europe at this time inspired a generation of performers, not only violinists, to explore new techniques on their own instruments. The pianists Fryderyk Chopin, Clara Schumann, Robert Schumann, Sigismond Thalberg, and Franz Liszt would each create a new, distinctive approach to the piano in the 1830s alongside contemporaries like Henri Herz, Ferdinand Hiller, and Ferdinand Ries.

Despite the brief disruption of the 1830 revolution, the Farrenc family continued to make music, to grow their business, and to expand their network of professional contacts beyond the borders of France throughout the 1830s. (Their daughter Victorine Farrenc was born in 1826. She would become Louise's star pupil; a gifted pianist and composer of songs, she was praised in the Parisian press for her performances of her mother's works as well as canonic works by Hummel and Beethoven, until she became debilitatingly ill as a teenager. She died in 1859, just thirty-three years old.) Although she did not engage in the career of a traveling virtuoso, Louise did travel with Aristide to England at least twice in the early 1830s, as we know from his letters to Hummel. Aristide mentions that Louise's performances there were well received and led to publication contracts. She may have accompanied him on trips to German and Austrian cities in these decades, too, to negotiate with publishers and connect with musicians who might perform her works, but documentation does not survive to confirm any further travel outside France.

By the late 1830s, Farrenc's compositions had begun to garner critical attention in France and abroad, which would bring new opportunities in the 1840s. In 1836, Robert Schumann included Farrenc's recently published *Air russe varié*, Op. 17, in an omnibus survey of nine variation sets by various composers. After typically acerbic comments about what he sees as the mediocre and vapid productions of the average virtuoso and a lukewarm assessment of works by Franz X. Chwatal and H. W. Stolpe, Schumann turns to Farrenc's variations. His paragraph provides unusually high praise, and it does so without qualifying his remarks by expressing surprise that they were composed by a woman (as many contemporaneous reviews would do throughout the 1840s). For these reasons, his review merits quotation in full:

If a young composer presented me with variations like those of L. Farrenc, I would highly praise him for his excellent faculties and the fine training which they bear witness to everywhere. I sought out soon enough the status of the author, namely the wife of the well-known music dealer in Paris, and I am annoyed that she is unlikely to find out about these encouraging lines. They are clean, sharp little studies, perhaps carried out under her teacher's eyes, but so sure in their outline, so intelligent in their execution, so complete, in a word, that one has to love them, even more so since a very gentle romantic scent wafts over them. As is well known, themes that allow for imitations are best suited for variation, and so the composer uses this to create all sorts of nice canonical games. She even manages to create a fugue, i.e., with reversals, diminutions, augmentations [*Umkehrungen, Engführungen, Vergrößerungen*] – and all of this is easy and melodious. I would only have wished for the ending to come in just as quiet a way as I suspected that it would, after what had gone before.[12]

Schumann identifies two traits that infuse almost all of Farrenc's mature compositions: Her propensity to create themes that lend themselves to learned manipulations of motives, which we might also link forward to developmental processes employed by Brahms and his generation in the later nineteenth century, identified by Arnold Schoenberg as "developing variation"; and her subtle mixture of Romantic elements within a Classically oriented work. Like many of her contemporaries and the slightly younger generation that Schumann represents, Farrenc's music conveys heightened drama through an expanded harmonic palette (compared to the music of Haydn and Mozart, for example) and a strong lyrical impulse, both of which impact her formal designs in the mature chamber music. Yet, Farrenc rarely took these innovative techniques to their extreme. Like other popular French composers of instrumental music in this transitional era, such as George Onslow, Farrenc found a "middle path" or *juste milieu* between the Classical styles or conventions of the past and the new techniques being explored by her most daring contemporaries, such as Hector Berlioz and Richard Wagner. We will return to the notion of the *juste milieu* shortly.

Farrenc performed her *Air russe varié* and several of her other compositions in a solo matinée concert at the Salle Pleyel in 1838. The critical response from established Parisians was similarly glowing. The anonymous reviewer for *La France musicale* described the *Air russe varié* as "unquestionably one of the outstanding works published in this genre," and noted that it "rises above the conventional form."[13] Antoine Elwart, writing for the *Revue et gazette musicale*, praised the composer's "vigorous" and "virile" style while noting that,

her double talent is tempered by a pure taste, the fruit of the diligent study that she has made of the works of the masters of her art. ... As a pianist, we have only praise to give to Mme Farrenc: The eight Études that she composed and performed on Sunday, as well as the grand variations on a theme from Comte de Gallenberg, show plenty of talent. One hopes that Mme Farrenc will continue to walk in the progressive track that she has entered so gloriously.[14]

The eight Études that Elwart mentioned represented a selection of numbers from Farrenc's *Trente Études* (published 1839). This major work would be one of her most important compositions of the 1830s because it solidified her reputation as a consummate musician of the modern day. It began to position Farrenc as a composer not only of fashionable works in genres associated with pianistic virtuosity, but also of learned pieces in a more "serious" or academic style. These pieces demonstrated her mastery of pianistic technique, compositional depth, and integration of modern harmonic and melodic tastes within a style that appealed to listeners with a variety of backgrounds. When Maurice Bourges, one of Paris's most influential critics, published a lengthy and detailed review of the Études in 1840, he suggested that they should be required study for all pianists.[15] That review alongside positive responses to performances of Farrenc's two concert overtures and her set of variations for piano and orchestra (the "Gallenburg" Variations, Op. 25) smoothed her transition from virtuoso pianist-composer to composer of chamber music and other works in "classical" genres.

Between about 1839 and 1850, Farrenc completed a series of chamber works that included two quintets for piano and strings (Op. 30 and Op. 31), two piano trios (Op. 33 and Op. 34), two sonatas for violin and piano (Op. 37 and Op. 39), and the Nonet for Winds and Strings (Op. 38). She also completed three symphonies in this period (Op. 32, Op. 35, and Op. 36), solidifying her reputation as a composer of serious music. After 1850, she would go on to write a sextet for piano and winds (Op. 40), a trio for clarinet with cello and piano (Op. 44), a trio for flute with cello and piano (Op. 45), and a sonata for piano and cello (Op. 46). All of these chamber works were published in her lifetime except the nonet and sextet. (The clarinet trio and flute trio were published with alternative violin parts to replace the wind instruments.) This body of works is the direct result of a change in priorities and musical ambitions at the end of the 1830s, for Farrenc individually and for musicians and audiences like her in Paris and beyond.

The Composer of "Serious" Music, 1840s to 1860

During the first three decades of the nineteenth century, the musical cultures of Europe gradually incorporated the principles of Romanticism into their artistic work and aesthetic, which led composers and musicians to create new genres, to expand their expressive horizons, and to develop new compositional techniques (like the expanded harmonic language, lyrical impulse, and longer, more complex forms pioneered by Schubert and Beethoven in the 1820s). The generation that came of age in the 1830s, including Robert and Clara Schumann, Fredyreck Chopin, Felix Mendelssohn, Franz Liszt, and Richard Wagner, led the charge in creating new genres to fulfill the Romantic desire to intermingle different art forms, or, to merge the poetic and painterly with the musical. In this, they followed the inspiration of writers and artists who had flourished a few decades earlier, at the turn of the century.

As a counterpart to the science- and reason-oriented philosophy of the Enlightenment, which dominated literary culture in much of the eighteenth century, philosophical and literary Romanticism privileged unfettered emotion, imagination, mystery, and spirituality. Romantics attempted to cast off conventional expectations and forms and to pursue what they considered more innate and personal styles in poetry, drama, and music. The movement began with writers and musicians like Jean-Jacques Rousseau (1712–1778) and Johann Gottfried Herder (1744–1803), who had both sought the origins of human culture in the arts and language of the past. Herder and Rousseau collected folk songs and created translations and pseudo-translations of poems and songs from throughout Europe, North America, and other colonized regions, an activity that would later provide materials and inspiration for fantastical exotic works depicting faraway lands and people with what were considered bizarre or barbaric social customs. They and their followers in the next generation of writers celebrated folk and indigenous cultures (for example, François-René de Chateaubriand's novels and theoretical writings about the "noble savages" of the Americas). Farrenc's choice of "a Russian air" for her Op. 17 set of variations is indicative of this newfound love of exotic folk materials; she also composed variations on Swiss and German themes (*Air Suisse varié*, Op. 7; *Variations sur un thème Allemand*, Op. 28) that capitalize on folklore's appeal with audiences and musicians.

Linked to this fascination with people and cultures living in a "natural" state – which is to say outside the strictures of formal aristocratic courts, the legal and economic responsibilities of cities, and other cosmopolitan bureaucracies – was a newfound reverence for the distant past, especially for the art and architecture of the Middle Ages, which led to new literary and artistic forms. French and German Romantics alike were inspired by new editions and translations of Shakespeare, Milton, and Dante, whose dark tragedies about human failings especially resonated with a generation of artists that came of age during or in the shadow of the Napoleonic wars. Gothic novels and poetic sagas explored the macabre and grotesque, the otherworldly, and unappreciated and lonely geniuses shunned by polite society but firm in their commitment to truth and art. Cornerstones of the literary movement include the epic poems of *Ossian* from the 1760s, Johann Wolfgang von Goethe's *The Sorrows of Young Werther* (1774, 1787) and *Faust* (1808, 1831), Lord Byron's *Childe Harold's Pilgrimage* (1812–18), and Walter Scott's *Ivanhoe* (1819), all of which inspired multiple musical works in the form of operas or music dramas, programmatic tone poems, sets of character pieces, and song settings throughout the nineteenth century.

Despite the popular appeal of Romantic themes and musical innovations, especially on the operatic stage, an influential group of critics and editors in Paris (and, to a lesser degree, in other cities throughout Europe and North America) found the new style too brash, too chaotic, and dangerous. Much as the leaders of the July Monarchy sought to find a workable compromise between the excesses of anarchy and absolutism, French critics supported composers exploring a middle way, or *juste milieu*, in instrumental music that would reinterpret the Classical past for the modern age without slipping into the extremes of Romanticism. Henri Blanchard summarized the taste of influential conservative critics in an 1845 review of a symphony in C minor by Carl Czerny that, to his ear, too closely imitated Beethoven's infamous model in the same key (his fifth symphony):

Between this imitation of beautiful models and the fanciful, the strange, the bizarre that those who use them alone take for originality, there exists, if we may be forgiven for this much-maligned word, a happy medium [*juste milieu*]. This eclecticism consists in the novelty of motifs, the simultaneously elegant and scientific working out of these motifs, and the use of all the riches of modern instrumentation that many composers now know best.[16]

Critics were not alone in their desire for a "middle way" or "happy medium" between Classicism and Romanticism, especially as an alternative to the programmatic music of Félicien David, Hector Berlioz, and Franz Liszt. In the 1840s, many composers and musicians who had been associated with the first wave of musical Romanticism turned their attention backwards in time and sought renewal in older forms and genres. Fryderyk Chopin gave one of his very rare public concerts in April 1841 at the Salle Pleyel, and afterwards began what Jim Samson calls "a reexamination of his artistic aims" that included close study of counterpoint treatises and increased perfectionism in his new compositions.[17] The 1840s also saw Robert Schumann turn from the art songs and idiosyncratic character pieces or musical miniatures for piano that had been his focus in the previous decade toward the symphony and chamber music. He produced his first two symphonies alongside other orchestral works and three string quartets, the piano quintet and piano quartet, two piano trios, and several other chamber works in this decade. In short, the 1830s had been characterized by the introduction and absorption of literary and philosophical Romanticism into musical life throughout central Europe, inspiring new approaches to composition and performance traditions as well as new genres. The 1840s, then, would be characterized by a return to earlier traditions and, for many composers, a dedication to infusing large-scale instrumental forms with this new Romantic aesthetic. The same tendency is evident in the works and activities of Louise Farrenc and her associates, particularly the women pianists who would cultivate an avid audience for chamber music in Paris during the 1840s (as we will see in greater detail in Chapter 1).

In the 1830s and 1840s, Paris also experienced a renaissance of instrumental music that critics and professional musicians, such as violinist and quartet leader Pierre Baillot (1771–1842), had been working to achieve for the previous two decades. New concert series for orchestral and chamber music took root, offering Parisian listeners a wealth of Classical and newly composed works. In 1828, the faculty and students of the Paris Conservatory, led by conductor François Habeneck (1781–1849), had founded an orchestral concert series under the auspices of the Société des Concerts du Conservatoire that set the tone for instrumental music-making in Paris throughout the nineteenth century. Habeneck, who led the orchestra until 1848, introduced the symphonies of Beethoven to Paris and helped to build an audience for these and other "serious" (Viennese Classical) works among concert goers. Subsequent groups and concert series sought to duplicate the success of that series in other musical arenas, and in later decades rival organizations such as Hector Berlioz's Philharmonic Society tried to counter what they saw as the overly conservative programming of the Conservatory concerts with new series of their own.

The flourishing of concert series created new opportunities for composers like Louise Farrenc, who turned her attention and compositional energy towards chamber music and the symphony around 1839 and largely abandoned the composition of piano showpieces for the next decade. (Her set of variations for four-hand piano duo on themes from Bellini's *I Capuletti*, Op. 29, was published by 1841 and probably composed around 1839–1840; it is the last work in that style by Farrenc. The piano music she published in the 1850s and early 1860s consists of sets of Études, Mélodies, and single-movement character pieces like the Nocturne, Op. 49, and the *Valse Brillante*, Op. 48.) In the wake of her successful 1838 solo concert and the positive reviews of her music by prominent critics, Farrenc composed two piano quintets for the popular Parisian instrumentation (piano, violin, viola, cello, and double bass) but using the Viennese four-movement structure with sonata forms in each of the outer movements.[18] Shortly after their publication, Georges Kastner reviewed these two works in a lengthy and detailed article in the *Revue et gazette musicale*.[19] Farrenc designed them with the Parisian public in mind and crafted the two quintets to demonstrate her compositional skill while also captivating listeners through virtuosic passagework for the piano, and they show her navigating the competing demands of critics and audiences during a transitional period in musical culture. Over the next ten years, Farrenc would continue to make judicious choices attuned to the needs and desires of her surroundings in three symphonies – each of which would be performed to critical acclaim in Paris and Brussels in the 1840s and 1850s, though they remained unpublished in Farrenc's lifetime – as well as two piano trios and two violin sonatas, all composed in the 1840s and published in the early 1850s.

Farrenc's reputation expanded in this era beyond that of a skilled pianist-composer with a sophisticated technique and taste, to include considerable renown as a teacher of music. In 1841 Helene von Mecklenburg-Schwerin, the Duchess d'Orléans (crown princess of France) engaged Louise Farrenc as a music teacher for herself and her children on the recommendation of the composers Fromental Halévy (1799–1862) and Daniel Auber (1782–1871); the latter was then serving as director of court concerts for the royal family. (Farrenc dedicated her second piano quintet to the duchess when it was published in 1842.) A year later, in summer 1842, Auber became director of the Paris Conservatory and offered Farrenc a position as Professor of Piano there. She began her thirty-year tenure at this institution in September 1842.

Farrenc excelled as a teacher of piano at the Conservatory, as demonstrated by the success of her students at competitions. The *Revue et Gazette musicale* published results of the Conservatory's annual exercises throughout the century, and Farrenc's pupils regularly finished in the top positions of their classes. In 1845, the piano department apparently adopted her *Trente Études* as a required component of the curriculum, further endorsing her role as a leading pianist and pedagogue.[20] Despite these affirmations, Farrenc was paid less than her male colleagues, including the pianist Henri Herz, who was hired in the same year and at the same rank, and the string players Jean-Delphin Alard and Auguste Franchomme, who were both hired after Farrenc. In November 1850, after the successful premiere and positive buzz generated by the Nonet for winds and strings and performances of her symphonies in Paris and abroad, Farrenc confronted Auber about this salary disparity and convinced him to raise her pay to equal that of her male colleagues (1,200 francs).[21] In her letter dated November 11, 1850, Farrenc notes that she had approached Auber about the salary disparity over a year earlier and now sought some definitive action from him on the matter. It seems that her persistence and the trajectory of excellence that she could now demonstrate were persuasive.

No artist works in a vacuum. This discussion has shown some of the ways that Farrenc's career responded to changes in musical culture from her piano-centric compositions and performances in the 1820s and 1830s to a more Classically oriented concert style in the 1840s and 1850s. Those changes connect to shifts in musical practice and the broader cultural context of Paris and its distinct musical institutions. Chapter 1 illuminates how Farrenc and her music, specifically the Nonet for winds and strings, reflect the specific activities of musicians in her inner circle and their efforts to sustain an audience for chamber music in Paris during the years surrounding the Revolutions of 1848.

Notes

1. For a discussion of the role that this ensemble (piano, violin, viola, cello, double bass) played in Parisian musical life, see Marie Sumner Lott, "Negotiation Tactics in Louise Farrenc's Piano Quintets, Opp. 30 and 31 (1839–40)" *Ad Parnassum* 8/15 (2010): 7–66.

2. Bea Friedland, *Louise Farrenc, 1804–1875: Composer, Performer, Scholar* (Ann Arbor: UMI Press, 1980); Catherine Legras, *Louise Farrenc: Compositrice de XIXe siècle: Musique au féminin* (Paris: L'Harmattan, 2003); Christin Heitmann, *Die Orchester- und Kammermusik von Louise Farrenc* (Wilhelmshaven: Florian Noetzel, 2004).

3. Heitmann, *Die Orchester- und Kammermusik von Louise Farrenc*, 18–25.

4. [Anon.], "Farrenc, Jeanne-Louise" in Fétis (ed.), *Biographie universelle des musiciens et bibliographie générale de la musique*, 2nd edn., vol. 4 (Paris: Didot Frères, 1866), 186–188. The entry is unsigned, but Farrenc's husband Aristide worked closely with Fétis on the *Biographie universelle*, suggesting he wrote this entry before his death in 1865. Farrenc's biographer Friedland identifies Jullien as the author in the main text of *Louise Farrenc* (259) but also points toward Aristide in a footnote (226, n.15).

5. Ralph Locke, "Paris: Centre of Intellectual Fervor," in *The Early Romantic Era: Between Revolutions: 1789 and 1848*, ed. Alexander Ringer (Englewood Cliffs: Prentice Hall, 1991), 32–83. On the role of opera in imperial nation-building, see M. Elizabeth C. Bartlet, "Politics and the Fate of 'Roger et Olivier,' a Newly Recovered Opera by Grétry" *Journal of the American Musicological Society* 37/1 (1984): 98–138; and Bartlet, "A Newly Discovered Opera for Napoleon," *Acta Musicologica* 56/2 (1984): 266–296.

6. Christin Heitmann, *Louise Farrenc: Thematisch-bibliographisches Werkverzeichnis* (Wilhelmshaven: Florian Noetzel, 2005), 100–101.

7. "Fantaisie pour flûte et piano composée et exécutée par M. et Mme Farrenc." Fétis, "Nouvelles de Paris" *Revue musicale* 3 (1828): 40–41.

8. "Aujourd'hui, à huit heures du soir, dans les salons de M. Erard, rue du Mail, no. 13, soirée musicale donnée par Mme Farrenc." Fétis, "Nouvelles de Paris" *Revue musicale* 2/2 (July 17, 1830): 346–347.

9. Katharine Ellis, "The Making of a Dictionary: François-Joseph Fétis, Aristide Farrenc, and the 'Biographie universelle des musiciens'" *Revue belge de Musicologie* 62 (2008): 63–78.

10. The Adagio that Fétis mentions was not announced in the program published on 17 July; Farrenc may have given it as an encore. "Cette jeune dame qui, par des études sérieuses, acquis sur le piano un talent fort distingué, a su résister au goût frivole qui a fait de cet instrument une mécanique, où l'agilité des doigts est seule remarquée, et dans laquelle il n'est point tenu compte du génie de l'artiste; elle a suivi la route tracée par Hummel, Moschelès, Kalkbrenner, et paraît destinée à y obtenir d'honorables succès. Elle s'est fait justement applaudir dans un septuor militaire inédit de Hummel, ainsi que dans un rondo et dans un adagio de ce maître." Fétis, "Nouvelles de Paris: Concert de Madame Farrenc." *Revue musicale* 2/2 (July 24, 1830): 376–377.

11. Katharine Ellis, "Female Pianists and Their Male Critics in Nineteenth-Century Paris" *Journal of the American Musicological Society* 50/2–3 (1997): 353–385.

12. "Legte mir ein junger Komponist Variationen wie die von L. Farrenc vor, so würde ich ihn sehr darum loben, der günstigen Anlagen, der schönen Ausbildung halber, wovon sie überall Zeugnis geben. Zeitig genug erfuhr ich den Stand des Verfassers, der Verfasserin nämlich, die die Gemahlin des bekannten Musikhändlers in Paris, und bin verstimmt, daß sie schwerlich etwas von diesen aufmunternden Zeilen erfährt. Kleine, saubere, scharfe Studien sind es, vielleicht noch unter den Augen des Lehrers vollführt, aber so sicher im Umriß, so verständig in der Ausführung, so fertig mit einem Worte, dass man sie lieb gewinnen muß, um so mehr, als über sie ein ganz leiser romantischer Duft fortschiebt. Themas, die Nachahmungen zulassen, eignen sich bekanntlich am besten zum Variieren und so benutzt denn dies die Komponistin zu allerhand netten kanonischen Spielen. Sogar eine Fuge gelingt ihr bis auf die, d.h. mit Umkehrungen, Engführungen, Vergrößerungen – und dies Alles leicht und gesangreich. Nur den Schluß hätt' ich in eben so stiller Weise gewünscht, als ich vermutete, daß es nach dem Vorhergehenden kommen würde." Robert Schumann, "Variationen für Pianoforte" *Neue Zeitschrift für Musik* 5/17 (August 26, 1836): 73.

13. *La France musicale* (May 27, 1838): 5. Quoted in Friedland, 22.

14. "Le style de madame Farrenc est fort et vigoureux; mais cette face toute virile de son double talent est tempérée par un goût pur, fruit des études sévères qu'elle a faites des oeuvres des maîtres de l'art. C'est avec plaisir que nous avons entendu les morceaux de musique vocale, [discussion of her *Dido abbandonata* setting and setting of Lamartine verses for chorus]. Comme pianiste, nous n'avons que des éloges à donner à madame Farrenc: les huit études qu'elle a composées et

exécutées dimanche, ainsi que ses grandes variations sur un thème du *Comte de Gallenberg*, prouvent beaucoup de talent. Espérons que madame Farrenc continuera à marcher dans la voie progressive où elle entre si glorieusement." A[ntoine] Elwart, "Concerts. De Mademoiselle Herminie Gebauer et Matinée de Madame Farrenc." *Revue et gazette musicale de Paris* 5/22 (June 5, 1838): 227–228.

15. Maurice Bourges, "Revue critique. Trente Études pour le piano, par madame Farrenc. ..." *Revue et Gazette musicale de Paris* 7/43 (July 5, 1840): 370–371.

16. "Entre cette manière imitative des beaux modèles et le fantasque, l'étrange, le bizarre que ceux qui les emploient prennent seuls pour de l'originalité, il existe, qu'on nous pardonne ce mot si décrié, un juste milieu. Cet éclectisme consiste dans la nouveauté des motifs, le travail tout à la fois elégant et scientifique de ces motifs, et l'emploi de toutes les richesses de l'instrumentation moderne que beaucoup de compositeurs connaissent maintenant au mieux." Henri Blanchard, "Revue critique. Première grande Symphonie en ut mineur et à grand orchestre, par Charles Czerny" *Revue et Gazette musicale de Paris* 12/38 (21 septembre 1845): 310. This review is also discussed in Ellis, *Music Criticism in Nineteenth-Century France: La Revue et Gazette musicale de Paris, 1834–1880* (Cambridge: Cambridge University Press, 1995), 163; Ellis provides an excellent introduction to the tenets of the *juste milieu* on pages 160–164.

17. Jim Samson, "Chopin, Fryderyk Franciszek" in *Grove Music Online* 2001 https://doi.org/10.1093/gmo/9781561592630.article.51099.

18. Sumner Lott, "Negotiation Tactics."

19. Georges Kastner, "Revue Critique. Premier et Second Quintette pour piano, violon, alto, violoncello, et contrebasse, par Mme L. Farrenc" *Revue et Gazette musicale* 10/2 (March 12, 1843), 96. See also Henri Blanchard 's review of the performance of the second quintet, which praises both works: Blanchard, "M. Lvoff – Madame Farrenc" *Revue et Gazette musicale* 7/61 (November 4, 1840), 521.

20. Friedland, 37 and 117.

21. The letter, translated in Friedland (p. 42), is preserved in the national archives of France: Archives du Conservatoire, Série AJ³⁷69⁽²⁾.

CULTIVATING AN AUDIENCE FOR CHAMBER MUSIC IN 1840s PARIS

On the evening of March 19, 1850, an eager audience of chamber music enthusiasts, critics, and fellow musicians gathered to hear a program of new music composed by pianist, composer, and Paris Conservatory professor Louise Farrenc at one of Paris's preeminent recital halls, the Salle Érard. Despite unseasonably warm weather that spring, the small concert hall was filled nearly to its capacity of 300 people in a mixture of reserved seats and standing-room spaces on the main floor, stretching from the rear of the hall right up to the small stage raised by just a step or two at the front of the narrow room. The two open galleries that lined the walls above provided additional seating for the evening's most esteemed guests. The candlelit room crackled with energy and an audible rustling of heavy silk as the assembled listeners waited eagerly for the concert to start. Slated to begin at 8:00 pm on a Tuesday evening, the concert was a major musical event, so the women would have donned fashionable evening dresses in richly patterned, colorful textiles with wide, bell-shaped skirts held up by stiff crinolines, and hoop skirts with whalebone supports. Their fitted bodices were made to show off bared sloping shoulders and a delicate waist (made possible by corsets that restricted their movement and enhanced an upright posture). Their elaborately coiffed hair with curls and braided loops hanging to both sides of their faces was left uncovered, and it invited the ladies to see and be seen in the hall, which would remain fully lit throughout the concert. The younger gentlemen in their midst would stand at the edges and back of the room for most of the concert. Older men or those with special, elevated status sat with their female companions. The men's appropriately bourgeois – which is to say, understated – tailcoats and trousers in shades of tan and brown provided a drab backdrop to the women's riot of color and texture. In the larger theaters of the day, men and women attending a play, opera, or concert might stroll about, visiting with friends and colleagues throughout the performance, and partaking in food and drink. Such events routinely lasted for several hours and formed an entire evening's entertainment. Tonight in the Salle Érard, though, the audience would be expected to listen more thoughtfully (and, perhaps, more quietly) to the music on offer. Tonight's performance would present only musical works composed by Madame Farrenc and only works in the serious or "classical" genres, signaling that the evening was designed for true connoisseurs of the best music, rather than for casual concert goers.

This semi-public event with its curated audience – the teaser announcement on March 3 said, "there's talk of a soirée *by invitation* to be given by Madame Farrenc"[1] – was an extension of the regular salon evenings that Farrenc held in her home throughout the year to perform a varied repertoire of piano and chamber music with her students. The music journals and newspapers of Paris frequently reported on these gatherings and the music played there, meaning that even music lovers who had been excluded were aware of Farrenc's reputation as a dazzling pianist and (much more surprisingly) as a learned composer in the classical style. Some of the audience members at this evening's event may have had the opportunity to hear Farrenc or her daughter Victorine play in other women's salon gatherings, as the Farrenc family participated in an active network of talented upper-class women devoted to making music together in appropriate semi-private spaces. These salon soirées typically featured the pleasing miscellany that nineteenth-century concertgoers expected and enjoyed, including one or more of Farrenc's own works, chamber music by Mozart, Weber, and Hummel, whose music (especially the glittering piano style and evocative wind parts of Hummel's septets) always pleased audiences, and some Beethoven (usually his early works, as the unfamiliar later style, with its dissonances and formal ambiguity, still unsettled even the most devoted fans of chamber music in Paris). Attendees at one of Madame Farrenc's soirées could also expect a fantasy or set of variations played by a virtuoso performer from the Conservatory, improvisations at the keyboard by the hostess or one of her talented pupils, popular songs and opera excerpts sung by guest performers, and, increasingly, examples of esoteric "ancient music" by Handel and Bach.

On this occasion, the audience in the Salle Érard was doubly energized by the opportunity to hear an exciting new piece of ensemble music – a nonet for winds and strings composed the previous year by the hostess and heard so far only by a small audience at a private salon gathering in December – and by the presence of a sensational new talent, a guest in Paris who had quietly conquered the local concert scene in the first few months of 1850. The young violinist Joseph Joachim, described as a virtuoso and a serious artist by all who heard him, was just eighteen years old and already concertmaster at the Leipzig Gewandhaus Orchestra and Professor of Violin at the conservatory there. He had been playing in Paris's salons since February. Although he had made a couple of appearances on benefit concerts at the bigger theaters, most of his performances had been in a series of chamber concerts taking place in this very hall with the respected Parisian pianist Thérèse Wartel (1814–1865) who had invited him and his countryman the cellist Bernard Cossmann to make an extended visit in Paris for that purpose.

The program for this concert had not been announced in the press beforehand. Attendees were aware that they would hear a selection of works composed by the hostess and that the newly composed Nonet for winds and strings would be performed "by Messieurs Joachim, Cossmann, and the elite of our artists."[2] Otherwise, it is unclear from a twenty-first-century perspective how much information listeners at the concert had as they waited for the musicians to step onto the raised platform at the front of the hall in the Salle Érard that night. Perhaps Farrenc's invitation to certain attendees included more information, or perhaps she had simply invited friends, colleagues, and patrons to come and enjoy an evening of exquisitely performed music in the exclusive company of musical connoisseurs. We can imagine the audience's excitement and the applause that greeted the pianist when she took her seat at the keyboard, joined on stage by Joachim and the cellist Charles Lebouc. (It could have been Cossmann, as the announcements had initially indicated, but Thérèse Wartel's review published the following week does not name him among the concert's participants.) They began with one of Farrenc's own piano trios. We don't know which one; two had been heard in Paris by the mid-1840s, but neither would be published until 1851–1852.

It's also not clear from later reports whether Louise Farrenc played the piano part in this trio or another pianist. Wartel's review, which is focused on the newly composed Nonet, states that the concert began with one of Farrenc's trios and ended with a sonata for piano and violin, also composed by Farrenc and played by Joachim. She says that "Madame Farrenc held the piano like a real composer," which could refer to the concert as a whole or just to her performance in the violin sonata.[3] The same issue of the *Revue et Gazette* – published on March 31, after Wartel's concert with Joachim and Cossmann on March 21 – includes a review by Henri Blanchard that mentions Farrenc, Wartel, and Charlotte de Malleville together, saying that all three "engaged with brilliant success in these charming musical conversations, the last two in the interpretation of the learned Nonet, the quintets, and the trios of the first."[4] The Nonet requires no pianist, which suggests that Blanchard may be recognizing Wartel's role in bringing the Nonet to the public (or that he misremembers the work). We know that Wartel performed Farrenc's piano quintet on March 21. Charlotte de Malleville (1829–1890) was a respected Parisian pianist who hosted a series of chamber concerts, four per year from 1849 to 1869; she frequently played Farrenc's chamber music both in these events and in other appearances. It is possible that she gave a different performance of a work by Farrenc at some point in March 1850 that is not documented in the available sources, or that she participated in Farrenc's March 19 concert.

These ambiguities abound in the surviving records about chamber music performances in nineteenth-century Paris and the players who participated in them. Modern scholars must piece together fragments of information from reviews, announcements, and the occasional letter, many of which contain puzzling errors (as in the Blanchard review and articles by various authors discussed later in this and subsequent chapters) or oblique references to musicians whose biographical details have often been lost to time. The performers of wind instruments in these and later performances prove difficult to trace because of such lacunae in the historical record, in part because wind music has received less scholarly attention than that for strings, piano, and orchestra.

This piano trio was almost certainly followed by a selection of shorter pieces for soloists, probably played by the wind soloists who had been engaged for the Nonet, and some songs for variety's sake, but these seem to have made no impression on the reviewers writing about the concert after the fact. The centerpiece of the event was clearly Farrenc's Nonet, a work that brought together nine virtuoso soloists – one each on flute, oboe, clarinet, bassoon, horn, violin, viola, cello, and double bass – drawn from Paris's most esteemed orchestras and theaters. In this performance, Joachim was joined by violist Adolphe Blanc, cellist Charles Lebouc, and bassist Achille Gouffé. The wind parts were played by flutist Louis Dorus, brothers Stanislas and Charles Verroust playing the oboe and bassoon, respectively, clarinetist Adolphe Leroy, and hornist Joseph-Francois Rousselot.

For many listeners in the audience, this group of performers would have been familiar. In addition to their regular appearances in orchestral concerts like those given by the Société des Concerts du Conservatoire (Society for Concerts of the Conservatory) and the Paris Opera, they were the core ensemble of the short-lived Society for Classical Music. Together, they had presented almost a dozen concerts in the past two years, each of which had contained a striking chamber work for wind instruments, including septets by Hummel and Alexander Fesca, wind quintets by Anton Reicha, nonets by George Onslow and Louis Spohr, and a *diecetto* for (ten) winds and strings, and Beethoven's quintet for piano and winds. Farrenc's concert must have seemed like a reunion of sorts, perhaps a bittersweet one, as the Society had effectively disbanded after their last few concerts in the previous season had failed to fill the hall. Unlike Farrenc's "by invitation" event, chamber series like those given by the Society for Classical Music or by the ad hoc ensemble of Wartel, Joachim, and Cossmann were open to members of the public, who could purchase tickets at their local music shops or by stopping in at the home of any of the players. The musicians organizing the concert had to rely on their own funds or on a combination of credit and favors to pay for the rental of the space and its facilities, music copying, printing or hand-copying of tickets, and so on, and then divide the income from ticket sales after all the bills were settled. In giving a "by-invitation" event, Farrenc was able to ensure donations from attendees or subscribers and to fill the hall with sympathetic listeners. Most of the musicians participated as a favor to the hostess, knowing that she would return it by playing without a fee when they hosted their own concerts. If the event went well and if critics and music lovers spoke highly of it, it would bolster later chamber concerts in the public eye and perhaps help to fill the hall for later series and concerts, ensuring financial and artistic success. If it faltered, that failure could have a domino effect on subsequent concerts of chamber music that season, not to mention on Farrenc's reputation with Paris's famously fickle public and beyond Paris, when Joachim and Cossmann returned to their homeland and shared their experiences with friends, family, and pupils. For Farrenc and her colleagues, an evening like this one that highlighted a single composer-performer was always a gamble.

In 1850, Paris had only recently begun to foster interest in and appreciation for "classical" chamber music, which had been deemed too cerebral and dry for French audiences only a couple of decades earlier. As a professional pianist and composer who was also a woman, Farrenc was an anomaly in her day – women had long been tolerated as performers in the private sphere, but only recently had they been able to break into the male-dominated world of public performance outside of the protected space of the domestic salon. As male critics had pointed out over and over again in the press, Farrenc's learnedness and skill as a composer were understood as highly unusual, even unique, in an age that believed most women to be incapable of sustained intellectual engagement or higher orders of thought.[5] Moreover, the headlining work on tonight's program was a nonet for winds and strings, a work that did not even utilize Farrenc's own instrument. She could not lead the ensemble from the keyboard and had, therefore, to put her trust in the young Joachim to lead an ensemble of players he had only just met.

In this chapter, I propose that Farrenc's choice to write a nonet for the 1850 season positioned her to continue supporting a vital network of chamber music performers and advocates at a crucial point in the development of Paris's chamber music culture. Throughout the 1840s, she had devoted all of her compositional energy to works in the "serious" or classical genres, writing three symphonies and a half-dozen chamber works in the Viennese style. Whereas orchestral performances required outside aid in the form of a (male) conductor willing to program an unknown work – keeping in mind that Farrenc could not, by convention, lead an ensemble on the public stage without risking her social status and reputation as modest, morally upright woman; that was an institutional privilege reserved for men alone – chamber music concerts allowed Farrenc to organize events herself by drawing upon her network of friends, colleagues, patrons, and students. Maintaining and growing the network of performers and patrons (audience members) for chamber music was an integral part of Farrenc's success as a professional musician, a responsibility that she took seriously and that she shared with a cadre of other talented professional and semi-professional women musicians based in Paris. These women, most of them pianists, carved out a niche for themselves in the world of professional music making by associating themselves with classical, learned chamber traditions.[6] Chamber music allowed them to play in public and semi-public spaces alongside men, but in ensembles that remained associated with domestic traditions cultivated in the home and salon. Operating within a social space that fell between "private" and "public" spheres, Farrenc and her allies were able to engage as professionals in a world that was often hostile to women taking agency outside the home.[7]

Promoting Chamber Music in Early Nineteenth-Century Paris

The year 1850 represents the culminating point in more than three decades of active promotion by performers, composers, and critics who sought to convince the Parisian public that chamber music was the most "pure" and elegant form of music making and one that deserved a hallowed place in Paris's public musical life with dedicated concert series and opportunities to hear the best examples of the style by Europe's most renowned composers. For critics and musicians looking to "elevate" French musical life by eschewing what they considered the empty virtuosity of the opera stage and solo concerto appearances, German (actually Viennese) chamber music offered a model to which composers and musicians should aspire. French critics in this era did not differentiate between "German" and "Austrian" composers or works. They described Beethoven, Mozart, and Haydn as German composers and their works as representative of a German ideal. When French musicians gave concerts in Vienna, French correspondents wrote of their success in "Allemagne" (Germany).

Since the 1820s, violinists like Pierre Baillot (1771–1842) and Jean-Delphin Alard (1815–1888) had cultivated a greater appreciation for the string quartet and related chamber genres among Parisian listeners by programming the works of Haydn, Mozart, Boccherini, Hummel, and Onslow alongside certain popular works by Beethoven in concerts devoted exclusively to chamber music. These concerts tended to center the Viennese Classical repertoire, which reflects French (and Austro-German) perceptions that these composers represented the chamber music ideal to which modern French musicians should aspire.[8] Perhaps best known today for his treatise *L'Art du violon* (1834) and his reputation as one of the late masters of the French Violin School, Baillot was also one of the most important chamber musicians of early nineteenth-century Paris. He established the city's longest-standing chamber concert series in 1814. For twenty-eight years, Baillot and a changing cast of colleagues presented a biweekly subscription-based series of concerts during the winter months. Each concert typically included three quartets or quintets for strings and ended with a solo work created and performed by Baillot as a sort of planned encore.[9] The subscribers to Baillot's series included aristocratic supporters, military and government officials, and members of the bourgeoisie, such as judges, bankers, professors or "men of letters," and business owners. Baillot also invited friends and professional colleagues, who received free tickets, including many musicians who went on to host their own chamber series following his model, like the brothers August and Théophile Tilmant; Charles, Arnaud, and Leopold Dancla (their sister Laure, a pianist and teacher of piano, played on their concert series as well); Anton and Max Bohrer; and the Müllers, a group of four brothers who formed a quartet as court musicians in their hometown of Braunschweig (Carl Friedrich, violin and leader; Franz Ferdinand, second violin; Theodor Heinrich, viola; and August Theodor, cello) and went on to perform in Paris in 1837, then throughout the world.

Jean-Delphin Alard was Baillot's spiritual and literal successor. (He was appointed professor of violin at the Paris Conservatory in 1843 following Baillot's death the previous year.) Like Baillot before him, Alard made his career as a multifaceted performer and teacher, playing in the orchestra of the Paris Opera and as a member and soloist in the concerts of the Society for Concerts of the Conservatory, while devoting considerable energy and resources to chamber music. Around 1835, he began offering chamber music concert series, first in a group with cellist Auguste Franchomme (1808–1884) as the Concerts du Cercle Musical and simultaneously in a short-lived collaboration with the cellist Pierre-Alexandre Chevillard (1811–1877) devoted to the performance of Beethoven's late quartets. (Chevillard's organization continued; it found a winning roster of musicians with Jean-Pierre Maurin and Sabbatier on violins and a Monsieur Mas on viola. This group performed to critical acclaim well into the 1870s.) Building on these models, chamber music societies flourished in the late 1830s and 1840s, with six separate groups offering distinct concert series in the 1839–1840 season and five in 1847–1848.[10]

After the innovations of Baillot, who retired in 1840, it was the women pianists of Paris who kept chamber music before the public's eyes and ears by programming string quartets or quintets and works for winds and strings alongside piano trios, quartets, and quintets by older and newer composers throughout the 1830s and 1840s, often specializing in music by Mozart and Beethoven. Louise Farrenc herself played a vital role in the rejuvenation of French instrumental music as a composer, teacher, performer, and concert organizer. Although she had always programmed works in a wide range of styles as a pianist, beginning in the late 1830s, Farrenc turned away from the virtuoso showpieces that she had used to establish herself on the musical scene and toward "serious" or classical genres. In the 1840s, she did not compose any new works for piano solo and concentrated instead on the orchestra and chamber music. Farrenc's music and that of her countryman George Onslow (who also focused on chamber music in this decade) were held up by critics and musicians as the best examples of modern serious French composition, and Farrenc and her pupils regularly programmed chamber music by Haydn, Mozart, Beethoven, and others, promoting a learned style that pleased audiences and critics simultaneously.

Although she is nearly forgotten today, pianist Thérèse Wartel also worked to facilitate a greater appreciation among French audiences for "classical" or "serious" music. She organized the Society for Classical Music and its concert series, which brought together the ensemble of wind and string players who inspired the composition of Farrenc's Nonet and later wind chamber music. Through her own performances and concert organizing activities, which were possible because of her reputation as a specialist in the performance of Beethoven and the Classical German repertoire, Wartel cultivated an audience for chamber music in Paris and supported the growing network of professional and semi-professional women musicians there. Wartel's activities within the overlapping musical circles of Leipzig, Vienna, and Paris link her and Farrenc to the various musicians who played in the successful public premiere of the Nonet in 1850. Although the Nonet does not employ the piano, its creation and premiere would not have been possible without Paris's network of professional women pianists and the performance opportunities that it fostered.

Thérèse Wartel and the "Cult of Classical and Severe Music"

Like Farrenc, Thérèse Wartel was a native Parisienne born into a family of artists and educated at the Paris Conservatory, where she won prizes in both piano and practical harmony in 1830. (Born Atale Thérèse-Annette Andrien, she was the daughter of the Flemish/Belgian bass Martin-Joseph Andrien [1767–1822], who sang at the Paris Opera between 1783 and 1804 and taught lyric declamation briefly at the Conservatory. Thérèse married the tenor Pierre-François

Wartel and the "Cult of Classical and Severe Music"

Wartel [1806–1882] in 1833; their son Louis-Émile was born in 1834 and grew up to become an important singer at the Théâtre Lyrique and then a singing teacher.[11]) In the 1830s, Wartel worked on the staff of the Paris Conservatory as an accompanist and teacher of solfège. Katharine Ellis notes that she was never elevated to the position of professor, which may explain why she left that role in 1838.[12] Also like Farrenc, Wartel excelled at navigating the difficult terrain of Paris's musical institutions while avoiding potential landmines created by the institutional misogyny of her day. She accomplished this by focusing her professional activities in the semi-public, semi-private salons of Paris and on chamber music, where her sensitive and nuanced renditions of works by respected composers of the classical school alongside some of Paris's most elite instrumentalists charmed both critics and audiences. With other women pianists who concentrated on chamber music, Wartel created space for women to engage in intellectual musical pursuits that were deemed appropriate for women and did not require them to compete with the more publicly oriented virtuoso careers of men like Sigismund Thalberg, Henri Herz, and Franz Liszt. Conservative critics who disliked the sensuous and over-the-top style of much modern pianism, with its expanded Romantic harmonies and noisy technical display, and who similarly disdained what they considered the inferior popular style of commercial "salon music" and vocal Romances that they associated with women composers and performers, nonetheless championed women pianists who played music by accepted masters of the earlier style: Mozart, early Beethoven, Hummel, and Weber. Critics frequently used the words "*sévère et classique*" or "*pur et sévère*" to describe both the performance styles of these women pianists and the music they valued, and that critics and connoisseurs associated with German Classicism and intellectual or musical rigor. Alongside Farrenc and Wartel, the pianists Clara Loveday, Charlotte de Malleville, Sophie Pierson-Bodin, and Louise Mattmann were all associated with classical repertoire and with chamber music performances, both as performers and as hostesses of salons and concerts. Unfortunately, beyond the activities of a few standout performers, such as Clara Wieck Schumann and Marie Pleyel, the wide network of female pianists active in the nineteenth century and their programming practices remain woefully under-researched.

Wartel, Farrenc, Loveday, and Malleville were frequently written about together as representatives of a new dawning of pianism. In 1845, the virtuosa Marie Pleyel returned to Paris to give concerts after having been away for more than ten years, and an anonymous writer for *Le Ménestrel* took the opportunity to note the prevalence of first-rate women pianists in the city:

Let us note that the year 1845 will mark a new era. – It is the revocation of Salic law [the exclusion of women from the line of succession] in the art of piano playing! A mighty army is already threatening the omnipotence of the beard. Mme Pleyel first; then the pianist of the queen of the French, Mme Catherine Dietz; the ladies Mattmann, Bohrer, Farrenc, Masson, Joséphine Martin, Loveday, Wartel, etc.; in short, a *ravishing* Pleiad which will easily prevail over a sex which in general has nothing ravishing about it.[13]

(In his public dedication, in 1844, of his *Reminiscences de Norma* to Pleyel, Liszt addressed Pleyel as his "dear and ravishing colleague" and noted cheekily that the work was "full of arpeggios, octaves, and dull platitudes, supposedly brilliant and extraordinary, with which many of our colleagues – much less ravishing, by the way – have been harassing us and murdering us for a long time."[14])

As noted earlier, Henri Blanchard's concert summary for the week of Farrenc's March 19 concert with the public premiere of the Nonet would mention a salon performance by Malleville, Wartel, and the public premiere of Farrenc's Nonet in the same sentence:

to come back to chamber music, which is in fashion this year, we must pay a just tribute of praise to Mesdames Farrenc and Wartel, as well as to Mademoiselle Charlotte de Malleville, who engaged with brilliant success in these charming musical conversations, the last two in the interpretation of the learned Nonet, the quintets, the trios of the first.

Blanchard continues by explaining how or why (in his view) women performers were so well suited to chamber music:

This handsome genre of music has replaced the French conversation of yesteryear, that the women directed and in which they are queens. [He means the salon gatherings that had been common at the turn of the century.] We have said so often that Madame Wartel is one of the most brilliant facilitators of this conversation, with the finesse and energy of her playing, with the intelligent time that she knows how to take, and who proves that she breathes and leads in a rational way with the fingers.[15]

Wartel had performed regularly with the best musicians of Paris in private and semi-public salons that attracted critical acclaim in the city's musical press throughout the late 1830s. By 1839, she was associated by critics with "good and pure" music. That year, she performed Beethoven's "Kreutzer" sonata for piano and violin with Jean-Delphin Alard on a Sunday concert of the Société musicale, a group modeled on the Concerts du Conservatoire series and formed specifically to raise public appreciation for classical chamber music. The program also included Mozart's D Major String Quintet. The reviewer of this performance noted that the sonata was "realized with precision, sharpness, and clarity. Madame Wartel lacks neither grace nor lightness; but, it must be said, we desired more than once the manly [mâle] and warm Lisztian energy that animates and vitalizes the whole. Monsieur Alard, for his part, was expressive and passionate."[16] Here and in other reviews of Wartel's playing, we see the double-bind that women faced in public performances and get a sense of why the smaller venues of the salon and recital hall suited her and many of her female colleagues so well. Male critics frequently noted a lack of "masculine power" and similar deficiencies in women's playing, but sometimes also criticized women when they "forgot" or abandoned their feminine delicacy and played too vigorously. For example, a critic in Vienna would later describe Wartel as "a pianist who possesses a very respectable ability, and stands at an unusual level in light, graceful performance; only now and then does her playing lack some manly power to give her performances real worth. She succeeds in all passages where by nature this aspect is not needed, and she won the undivided approving recognition of the public."[17] In March 1844, though, Blanchard welcomed her return to Paris with a review that noted "A concerto by Bach, a beautiful work by Beethoven, and the brilliant salon piece by Weber offered her the opportunity to show a severe, solid and even masculine talent, without force, brilliance and verve making her forget the grace inherent in her quality as a pretty woman."[18] Wartel would go on to perform Beethoven's music regularly in subsequent decades, and she would write a well-received book on interpreting Beethoven's piano sonatas that was published just before her death in 1865.[19]

Wartel's reputation as a leader in the world of chamber-music performance, and thus her ability to organize well-attended and respected concert series, was burnished by the success of her performances during a tour of German-speaking cities during the early 1840s, which gave her an opportunity to perform German music before German audiences. In July 1842, Thérèse and her husband, the opera singer François Wartel, left Paris for an extended performance tour that started in Vienna and would take them to Prague, Pest, Leipzig, and Berlin. (They may also have visited Dresden and Petersburg after leaving Vienna, as an announcement of their travel plans suggested in March 1843, but I have not found reviews of appearances in those cities.) On their joint concerts and recitals, François sang German *Lieder* (art songs) by Beethoven and Schubert in French translations as well as French *romances*. Thérèse distinguished herself in the eyes and ears of local critics by consistently including works by Bach and Beethoven in her programs alongside popular showpieces by C. M. von Weber and her own virtuoso compositions, such as a fantasy on motives from Meyerbeer's *Les Huguenots* and a Caprice "in Thalberg's manner," according to a review from November 1842. During this tour, Thérèse is never described as accompanying her husband, and some reviews specify that François sang with a local pianist. Thérèse performed solo and chamber works on the couple's joint recitals and in her own solo appearances with local musicians, building a network of performer friends that she could rely on in the future. In Vienna, for example, she was accompanied by a violinist Herr Mayer in at least two concerts featuring a movement from a Beethoven sonata for piano and violin, and by him and cellist Herr Bagge for a performance of a piano trio in B flat by Beethoven (Op. 97, the Archduke). Her performances on this tour, though, were not limited to chamber music; she also played Weber's *Konzertstück* and Beethoven's E Flat Concerto with the orchestra of the Vienna Musikverein.

Significantly for Thérèse's future musical connections, the same concert season in which the Wartels performed in Vienna (winter of 1842–1843) saw a well-publicized series of concerts featuring the child superstar violinist Joseph Joachim (eleven years old at the time), who was finishing his first and last year as a student at the Vienna Conservatory. In spring 1843, when the Wartels spent a few weeks in Leipzig, Joachim traveled to this city for his interview and audition to study with Felix Mendelssohn at the newly founded Leipzig Conservatory. (They would have missed Joachim's April 30th debut at the Vienna Musikverein.) While in Leipzig and Berlin in May and June 1843, Thérèse Wartel met and made music with Mendelssohn and members of his circle. Mendelssohn's brother-in-law Wilhelm Hensel made a drawing of Thérèse that she then inscribed, thanking him and his wife Fanny Mendelssohn Hensel for their hospitality and thanking the latter, especially, for the enjoyable hours they spent together at the piano.[20] The only public report of the Wartels' concerts in this part of the tour comes from Berlin, where Thérèse played the Andante with variations from Beethoven's Sonata for Piano and Violin in A Minor, Op. 23, with Leopold Ganz.[21] The Wartels returned to Paris in 1843, and, in the spring of 1844, reviews of Thérèse's performances mention that she "has just traveled through Germany" and that she had been applauded enthusiastically there.[22] Having effectively established herself as an authority on the classical, serious, chamber style associated with Beethoven and other German artists of the earlier generation, Wartel returned to her concertizing in Paris with renewed clout and an even greater sense of having a special relationship to the chamber music repertoire.

Meanwhile, the German cellist Bernhard Cossmann (1822–1910), who would collaborate with Wartel, Joachim, and Farrenc in the Nonet performance and other chamber concerts in 1850, had moved to Paris in 1840 as an eighteen-year-old virtuoso. He played for several years in the orchestra of the Théatre-Italien, but from about 1846 he was able to make a living from concert appearances without a regular job as an orchestral player by dividing his time between winters in Paris and summers in the spa town of Baden-Baden (located just over the border, on the German side of the Rhine river, it was the preferred summer playground of rich Parisians), where he expanded his circle of patronage and musical collaborators. In April 1844, Cossmann gave a solo recital in Paris featuring transcriptions of Schubert melodies, a fantasy on themes from Meyerbeer's *Robert le Diable*, and a fantasy based on Weber's *Der Freischütz*. Thérèse Wartel, still enjoying the critical glow that lingered from her tour in Germany, played "the salon concerto" by Weber accompanied by string quartet on this recital, which may be the first instance of her fruitful collaboration with Cossmann.[23]

A few months later, Cossmann and Wartel played together at the first gala concert sponsored by the *Revue et Gazette musicale de Paris*, where they offered a duo by Felix Mendelssohn for piano and cello. The review of this performance shows how difficult it was at the time to strike a pleasing balance between serious or learned styles and lighter, more brilliant styles for the Parisian public, and it demonstrates Wartel's savvy navigation of those difficulties. The review by Blanchard begins with a paean to the classical learnedness of chamber music:

Here it is again, this exhibition of classical quartets, this good *musica da camera*, these sessions which have been nicknamed the sisters of those of the Conservatory with their devoted following and known under the name of the Société des Concerts: there we find the core of those faithful to the true principles of art; there artists, amateurs who do not allow themselves to be stunned by the hustle and bustle, the wantonness of the so-called musical press, form the audience for these sessions. This public never applauds inappropriately, because it analyzes what is given to it.[24]

The remainder of the review makes clear, though, that the audience at even this type of event required variety and levity between serious pieces and preferred a balance of the two within them, if possible. The program began with Beethoven's String Quartet, Op. 59/3, which Blanchard described as beginning "with the most strange harmonies, with chords with unexpected resolutions; it would be musical Romanticism if the regularity, the unity of thought were not to immediately testify that it was not a momentary whim of genius."[25] This challenging work was followed by excerpts from operas by Donizetti and Bellini sung by a Mademoiselle Grevedon and a selection of songs in French sung by Madame Laty. Then Wartel and Cossmann took the stage:

In the cult that she dedicated to classical and severe music, Mrs. Wartel, seconded by Mr. Cossmann, performed the second duet, for violin and cello [sic[26]] by Mendelssohn, a piece of arid science, far too labored, and which was addressed above all to contrapuntists who are not numerous enough in France to form an audience for it. Be that as it may, the pretty and skillful pianist showed us there, as always, her nimble, accentuated, brilliant and warm execution. But we preferred to find these qualities in an Étude of her composition, and dedicated to Thalberg, which was not announced on the program, and which she gave us in compensation for the overly scholastic piece she had performed with Mr. Cossmann, one of our finest cellists.[27]

Wartel's decision to add a virtuoso showpiece of her own to the program after the Mendelssohn duo demonstrates her clear understanding of Parisian tastes. Although she was lauded by critics and audiences as a performer of serious music, she frequently softened the effect of this "severe" repertoire with pieces that sparkled with technical brilliance and allowed her to display a singing melodic style, such as fantasies on operatic tunes and works by Weber or Hummel. The concert closed with a string quartet by Mozart, whose music easily bridged the divide between the serious, "German" chamber style and the Italianate melodiousness that French audiences craved. (Louise Farrenc's chamber music was often favorably compared to Mozart in these decades, as his works were held up as the gold standard of elegance by critics and performers alike.)

When Cossmann visited Berlin and Leipzig on a tour in 1846, he met Felix Mendelssohn, who invited him to take up a position at the Leipzig Gewandhaus Orchestra. There, he and the young violinist Joseph Joachim played many concerts and chamber evenings alongside the cadre of top-notch players engaged at the Gewandhaus and Conservatory. After Mendelssohn's early death in 1847, the musicians of Leipzig experienced not just the loss of their friend and colleague, but a terrible vacuum created by his sudden absence in the city where he had been concert music's driving force. While Cossmann traveled to Baden-Baden and London during the revolutionary upsets of 1848–1849, Joachim sought out new options for his musical future. In a letter to his brother in March 1848, he said that he could not possibly go to Paris because he did not know anyone there "with whom I wish to be associated, although there are plenty I should prefer to keep at a distance."[28] During his formative years in Vienna and in Leipzig, Joachim had absorbed an aversion to virtuosity and salon music which he and others considered empty, facile displays of sentiment and technique devoid of poetry and which many German critics associated with the virtuoso culture of Paris. No letter survives to clarify when or how Joachim changed his mind, but by December 1849, he and Cossmann were on their way to Paris together, where they played in a series of chamber concerts and salon performances with Thérèse Wartel and other local musicians. It seems to have been at Wartel's invitation that they traveled to Paris in the first place. Over two decades later, in 1871, a biographical sketch of Cossmann noted that he "went to Paris with Joachim to give chamber music soirees with this master and Thérèse Wartel at the Salle Érard."[29] Cossmann and Joachim gave concerts with many musicians during their trip, including the German piano virtuoso Jakob Rosenhain (1813–1894), who had made his home in Paris since 1849. That this author singled out Wartel suggests her importance in planning the string players's trip to Paris as well as the respect she continued to command among music lovers six years after her death. More pertinently for our purposes here, it was almost certainly her influence that led Cossmann and Joachim to the music of Louise Farrenc.[30]

It is not clear from surviving records whether Thérèse Wartel knew Louise Farrenc personally before 1845, but she must have been aware of the elder composer and her music, as Farrenc's works and her piano playing had been well reviewed in the French press since the early 1830s, and (as discussed earlier) the two pianists were frequently mentioned together by critics like Henri Blanchard and Maurice Bourges in notices that described the women as paragons of good taste working to raise the quality of musical fare available to Parisian listeners. Farrenc had presented successful concerts in London in 1832 and 1833, and her activities as a performer and composer had accelerated considerably in the 1840s with the publication and glowing reviews of her piano quintets, opp. 30 and 31, the *Hymn russe varié*, Op. 27, and her *Trente Études*, Op. 26.[31] By 1845, all three of her symphonies had been performed in public concerts in Paris and in Brussels with favorable reviews in the French press, which surely would have caught the attention of a musician like Thérèse Wartel. Regardless, the first documentation we have of contact between the Wartels and the Farrencs is a concert report from July 1845, when François

Wartel performed in one of Farrenc's matinée concerts, in which nineteen-year-old Victorine Farrenc played her mother's Piano Quintet No. 2. Farrenc's second Piano Trio, Op. 34 in D minor, was heard on this concert as well (possibly performed by Louise Farrenc).[32] Five years later, Thérèse Wartel played the second quintet with Joachim and Cossmann in their March 21 concert alongside works by Bach, Beethoven, Mozart, and Mendelssohn. When Farrenc published the D minor Trio in the early 1850s, she dedicated it to Thérèse Wartel, who reciprocated with the dedication of her *Andante cantabile* for piano, Op. 11, "à Madame Louise Farrenc" when it was published in 1851.

By 1849–1850, the proponents of chamber music in Paris had succeeded, and the city had developed an enthusiastic audience ready to enjoy and support a variety of works in the "serious" genres by both German-born and native composers. This expansion of musical taste was possible, in part, through the professionalization of chamber music performance, which brought chamber music out of the home and into the concert hall alongside works for piano and winds, winds and strings, and other configurations. Then as now, musicians and audiences embraced the semi-public, semi-private nature of chamber music and the intimate musical experiences it facilitated, compared to the opera or symphony concerts. That said, the need to temper the "serious" or "severe" style of chamber music with works that provided greater variety continued to be a concern for concert promoters. Baillot had offered a virtuosic showpiece at the end of his concerts to fulfill that wish, and subsequent performers tended to include one or more sets of variations or fantasies in a more or less virtuosic style mid-concert as a sort of palate-cleansing work. Some chamber concert organizers of the later 1840s found that Classical or classically inspired works for wind instruments provided a welcome novelty and variety between works for strings alone or piano and strings, without "compromising" the serious tone of the event. Thus, chamber music in Paris embraced the "petite symphony" ideal of works for a mixture of seven, eight, and even ten wind and string players.

Prior to 1849, Farrenc had not composed or published any works featuring wind instruments, despite the fact that her husband Aristide was a flutist and composer of flute music and that she had been teaching alongside some of Paris's finest wind players at the Conservatory since 1842. Other than her highly acclaimed solo piano works, she had composed only for orchestra, for voice, and for piano with strings. Her turn to the large chamber ensemble for winds and strings seems to have been made in response to the successful concerts put on by the Society for Classical Music, in 1847–1848 and 1849.

The Society for Classical Music

In 1847, Wartel and eleven associates established the Society for Classical Music to give a series of chamber soirées in Paris in alternation with the Société de Concerts du Conservatoire, which was the leading organization for orchestral music in the city. In his book on chamber music concerts in nineteenth-century Paris, Joël-Marie Fauquet says that the society was formed "presumably at the instigation of Théophile Tilmant" without further evidence.[33] Though certainly the violinist and conductor was an important founding member and may have been central to the Society's success, Wartel clearly played a, perhaps *the*, leading role in organizing and running the society, given her lifelong activity as a concert organizer. The series of chamber concerts that she facilitated during Joachim's and Cossmann's tour in Paris, for example, bears all the hallmarks of a tireless administrator, and one who had to make opportunities for herself because she could not earn a living as a conductor, concert master, or court musician. (Louise Farrenc similarly had to arrange opportunities for her music and her students, the majority of whom were women, to be heard in private and semi-public spaces, and to rely on men to advocate for and perform her orchestral works.) Wartel's name was inextricably linked to the Society, as when Blanchard reviewed one of its concerts in January 1848: he started by calling it "the concert of chamber music given by Madame Wartel and her co-associates in the Salle Herz."[34] The Society facilitated public performances of popular chamber music in Paris with a regular, recurring series of concerts intended to offer Parisian listeners a wide selection of repertoire drawn from the roster of what were then considered master composers of the classical style, such as Hummel, Onslow, and Spohr, alongside Mozart, Beethoven, and Haydn. Like other societies formed in the shadow of the Société des Concerts du Conservatoire, Wartel's group sought to "do for chamber music what the celebrated society that reigns at the Conservatoire has done for the symphonic masterpieces."[35] Its founding members included Théophile Tilmant with his brother the cellist Alexandre (the Tilmant brothers also hosted their own string quartet concert series from 1833 until 1849, when Théophile became principal conductor for the Opéra-Comique), violinist Auguste-Antoine Guerreau, Paris's leading violist Louis Casimir Ney, and the Paris Opéra's star double bassist Achille Gouffé. All of these string players had been associated with performances of chamber music focused on the classical traditions in their own series of private and public concerts. The wind players likewise represented the most in-demand chamber players and soloists in Paris, many of whom were already teaching at the Conservatory and/or employed as regular members of the Concerts du Conservatoire orchestra: flutist Louis Dorus, who was an early adopter of the new Boehm design for the instrument that would become the modern standard; oboist Stanislas Verroust and his brother the bassoonist Charles; clarinetist Hyacinthe Klosé; and hornist Joseph-François Rousselot. Wartel's brother-in-law, the singer and actor François Delsarte (who also hosted a salon in which both Wartel and Farrenc regularly performed) and his students provided vocal selections at the Society's concerts.

This star-studded ensemble would introduce the Parisian public to both newly created works, like the Nonets of Farrenc and Onslow, and older pieces, some of which had never been performed in Paris, alongside crowd-pleasing favorites. From its first concert, the Society favored works for winds and strings, capitalizing on Parisian audiences's love of novelty and variety. The focus on wind music differentiated their performances from the earlier concert series of violinist Pierre Baillot and contemporaneous series headed by string players. Works for mixed ensembles had long been more popular in France than homogeneous ensembles like the string quartet. For example, Franz Liszt wrote to Robert Schumann in 1839 encouraging him to compose some ensemble music (trios, quintets, and septets) that he offered to introduce to audiences in Paris because "I am convinced that success, even commercial success, would not be wanting" in Paris, "where that sort of composition, when well played, has more chance of success than you perhaps think."[36] Two of the most frequently performed works on chamber concerts in Paris during the nineteenth century were Beethoven's Septet in E Flat Major, Op. 20, for clarinet, horn, bassoon, violin, viola, cello, and double bass (1802) and Hummel's Septet in D Minor, Op. 74, for piano, flute, oboe, horn, viola, cello, and double bass (1816). Hummel's *Septuor militaire*, Op. 114, for piano, flute, clarinet, trumpet, violin, cello, and double bass was also very popular in this era. (Aristide and Louise Farrenc programmed this work, which was then unpublished, on their 1830 concert on which the composer also performed.)

The Society for Classical Music programmed at least one work for winds on each of its concerts in the 1847, 1848, and 1849 seasons. (See Table 1.1.) Because the Society had programmed the Nonets by Louis Spohr and George Onslow the previous two seasons, it is probable that Farrenc also originally conceived her work for this group of players, anticipating that they would program it during their fourth season in 1850. She had collaborated on earlier occasions with several of the group's founding members. In her March 1849 salon concert, she played a flute sonata by Friedrich Kuhlau with Dorus on a program that included her own piano trio and one of her piano quintets. (The string players are not named in Blanchard's review, which describes Farrenc's trio and quintet as "like those of Mr. Onslow, in the manner of our great masters, with the graceful inspirations and the serious knowledge which characterize the talent of this composer and virtuoso pianist, licensed in fugue and counterpoint."[37]) Achille Gouffé played Farrenc's piano quintets on several occasions and is reported to have played the first quintet in October 1849 with pianist Delphine Barraud, making it likely that he had participated in Farrenc's soirée the previous March. Théophile Tilmant had conducted the orchestra when one of her overtures was played at a benefit for the Society of Artist-Musicians in 1845. In short, though Farrenc was not a member of the Society for Classical

44

Table 1.1 *List of works performed by the Society for Classical Music (listed in Joel-Marie Fauquet,* Les sociétés de musique de chambre à Paris de la Restauration à 1870*).*

1847	* *indicates a Paris premiere*
November 28	Mozart, String Quartet (K. 458 [?])
	Mendelssohn, Piano Trio, Op. 49
	Spohr, Nonet for Winds and Strings, Op. 31
December 12	Beethoven, Piano Trio, Op. 1 No. 3
	Mozart, Clarinet Quintet, K. 581
	Hummel, Septet for Piano, Winds, and Strings, Op. 74
December 26	Beethoven, Quintet for Piano and Winds, Op. 16
	Haydn, String Quartet, Op. 77 No. 2
	Mozart, String Quintet
	Hummel, Flute Trio, Op. 2a No. 1
1848	
January 16	Beethoven, String Quartet, Op. 18 No. 5
	Mozart, Clarinet Trio, K. 498
	Onslow, String Quintet, Op. 67
	* Fesca, Septet for Piano, Winds, and Strings, Op. 26
January 30	Haydn, String Quartet, Op. 76 No. 2
	Reicha, Wind Quintet
	Bach, Keyboard Concerto, BWV 1052
	Hummel, Quintet for Piano and Strings, Op. 87
Planned	*Beethoven, String Quartet, Op. 18 No. 6*
February 13	*Mendelssohn, trio*
	* *Spohr, Octet for Winds and Strings, Op. 32*
Planned	*Beethoven, Serenade, Op. 25*
February 27	*Haydn String Quartet*
	Mozart, Quintet for Piano and Winds, K. 452
	Bach, Keyboard Concerto, BWV 1052 (encored)
Planned	*Beethoven, Piano Trio, Op. 97 (?)*
March 11	*Beethoven, Septet for Winds and Strings, Op. 20*
	Onslow, String Quintet, Op. 72
	Bach, Sonata for Piano and Violin
1849	
February 4	Beethoven, String Quartet, Op. 18 No. 1
	Mozart, Piano Quartet, K. 478
	Reicha, Diecetto for Winds and Strings
February 25	Beethoven, Clarinet Trio, Op. 11

Table 1.1 (*cont.*)

	Haydn, String Quartet
	Reicha, Wind Quintet
	Bach, Keyboard Concerto, BWV 1052
March 11	Haydn, String Quartet
	Mozart String Quartet, K. 499
	Reicha, Wind Quintet
	Hummel, Septet for Piano, Winds, and Strings, Op. 74
March 25	Beethoven, String Quartet
	Mozart, Trio
	* Onslow, Nonet for Winds and Strings, Op. 77
	Bach, Sonata for Piano and Violin
April 9	Beethoven, String Quartet, Op. 130
	Mozart, String Quintet, K. 581
	Reicha, Wind Quintet
	Mendelssohn, Piano Trio, Op. 49
April 13	Beethoven, Septet for Winds and Strings, Op. 20
	Mozart, Sonata for Piano and Violin
	Reicha, Wind Quintet
	Bertini, Nonet for Winds and Strings, Op. 107

Music and they did not program her music during their two seasons of operation, she was an important member of the network of musicians that it supported.

In late 1849, Louise Farrenc offered a sort of "soft premiere" (perhaps actually a dress rehearsal) to promote her new work for winds and strings. In November, the news section of the *Revue et Gazette musicale* announced that "Madame Farrenc has just completed a Nonetto for string and wind instruments. This new composition will be performed this winter by the first-rank artists in Paris."[38] The first performance of the work occurred on December 23, 1849, at the salon of Sophie Pierson-Bodin (the pianist and teacher to whom Farrenc's *Trente Études* had been dedicated at their publication in 1839), where the Nonet was played by an ensemble comprised primarily of musicians from the Society for Classical Music. Guerreau and Charles Lebouc substituted for the Tilmant brothers on violin and cello respectively, but the remainder of the group was the same ensemble that Paris chamber-music enthusiasts had come to know in the

Society's concerts: Casimir Ney on viola, Gouffé on double bass, with Dorus, the Verroust brothers, Klosé, and Rousselot playing the wind parts. Most of these members also participated in the public premiere of the Nonet at the Salle Érard in March the following year, when Joachim took over the violin part.[39] Just as Hummel's participation in Aristide and Louise Farrenc's soirée in 1830 had ensured a large and appreciative audience for one of their earliest musical presentations, Joachim's presence on Farrenc's concert in March 1850 guaranteed that the Salle Érard would be full when the Nonet made its public debut.

In 1850, Paris was buzzing with news of the "German violinist" who had arrived with Cossmann in January. Joachim – who was actually Hungarian; he had spent his early childhood in Pest and then studied in Vienna before moving to Leipzig to study with Mendelssohn in 1843 when he was twelve years old – performed in several salons, according to an anonymous writer for the "Nouvelles" section of the *Revue et Gazette musicale*, who noted,

We have had this week the occasion to hear him in some salons, and we would like to affirm that his fame has not been exaggerated. Monsieur Joachim is not only an astonishing virtuoso, who, for example, performed on his own a fugue in four parts by Bach; he is an artist in the highest sense of the word, who interprets with a deep sentiment the Morceaux by Ernst, the concertos of Beethoven and of Mendelssohn, the quartets of the great masters. In sum: all that can be called great and good music.[40]

Like Wartel and Farrenc, Joachim's connection to "good music" distinguished him from the "frivolous" technical displays associated with virtuosos by critics of the day, and his insistence on performing the older repertoire, especially the music of Bach, showed him to be an artist interested in the learned traditions and intellectual enrichment that they represented.[41] For Joachim, the added benefit of the technical difficulty involved in realizing Bach's counterpoint on a single instrument usually associated with linear melodic parts allowed him to combine learnedness with a dazzling display of skill that audiences clearly enjoyed. Katharina Uhde has shown that Joachim's performance activities, especially his focus on German repertoire, in the 1850s demonstrate "his evolving views on what it meant to be an artist" and "a growing reluctance to be associated with Hungarians at a time when … there was a certain hostility toward former Hungarian revolutionaries."[42]

Joachim's performances in chamber concerts with Wartel and Cossmann (and Farrenc) allowed him to deepen his public commitment to "serious" music and to a "Germanic" persona while building connections to like-minded musicians abroad. During the twelve weeks that Joachim spent in Paris in 1850, he played in eleven concerts advertised or reviewed in the press, in addition to performances in salons and private gatherings (only some of which leave traces in the journalistic record, as in the Nouvelles announcement cited earlier in this chapter). Of those eleven concerts, eight were devoted to chamber music (and song) exclusively. The other three were larger events such as Blanchard's concert organized for the relief of the poor and the first concert of Berlioz's newly formed Philharmonic Society. For two of these Joachim still played chamber works. For Blanchard's concerts on January 28 and March 17, he played a Beethoven piano trio with Jakob Rosenhain and Cossmann and then presented Heinrich Wilhelm Ernst's *Fantaisie brilliant* on themes from Rossini's *Otello*. He also played the latter work on Berlioz's concert, which is the only documented appearance in which he did not play chamber music during his time in Paris. (The surviving press offers no indication that he performed his own compositions, though he might have done so in private performances, or the Beethoven and Mendelssohn concertos that he had already performed to such acclaim in London and elsewhere.)

Having determined, probably after persuasive conversations and correspondence with Cossmann and Wartel, that a trip to Paris could further his agenda as a performer of great works from the canon of classic repertoire and that the city did, in fact, play host to musicians worth knowing, Joachim seems to have made it his mission while in Paris to give only public performances that aligned with those values. Thérèse Wartel, Louise Farrenc, and their overlapping circle of friends and collaborators had been pursuing similar goals in Paris throughout the 1840s. Together, they built a culture for chamber music performance and

48

appreciation in a city that had long been regarded as interested only in the razzle-dazzle of opera and virtuoso performances.

As with most stereotypes, though, Paris's reputation as a center for spectacular, sensuous excess held a kernel of truth. Paris's most long-lasting contribution to nineteenth-century musical culture in Europe was its warm reception of virtuoso concert performers – the city excelled at making these performers feel like superstars and offered unparalleled opportunities for virtuosos to hone their craft and to monetize their talent – and its passion for operatic extravagance as best demonstrated in the genre of French Grand Opera. ("Grand Opera" refers to the specially conceived repertoire in fashion at the Paris Opéra in the 1830s and 1840s: fully sung music dramas with spectacular staging and grandiose proportions, usually with five acts, rather than the three typical in other theaters, and often highly melodramatic with violent and tragic plots, often historical and/or exotic in style.[43]) The activities of Wartel, Joachim, Cossmann, and Farrenc demonstrate the balance that was required for artists to be financially successful in a culture that continued to value ear-catching novelty, even if an ardent group of connoisseurs sought to sustain an audience for "serious" music. The dissolution of the Society for Classical Music after just two seasons (successful though they were critically and musically) demonstrates, too, the precarious nature of concertizing as a vocation. Both Maurice Bourges and Henri Blanchard noted the impact of political events on musical ones in their February 1849 reviews of the Society's first concert of that season. Bourges highlights the surprising proliferation of chamber music societies just before the disruptive revolutions of February and June 1848:

If the conflict of so many tumultuous events crammed into a single year has not entirely baffled the memory of our readers, they will doubtless recall that at the beginning of the last musical season, from November 1847 to February 1848, there appeared in Paris a sympathetic tendency, altogether unaccustomed, in favor of instrumental chamber music. Societies which proposed to offer exclusively to their subscribers trios, quartets, quintets, etc., arose in notable numbers, and, surprisingly, found people who would listen.

At the height of this active germination, for the first time appeared the [Society for Classical Music]. ... From the first session, dated November 28,

1847, the liveliest interest was attached to these meetings, which a very special public, a public of connoisseurs, facilitated with their patronage. But February broke like lightning. Suddenly reduced to silence by the formidable tutti of political clamor, this nascent institution had to fade away like many others, while waiting for better days.[44]

The years immediately following the establishment of the short-lived Second Republic in 1848 saw Prince-President Louis-Napoleon Bonaparte consolidate power in the executive branch of the newly formed government, introduce new voting restrictions to disenfranchise workers, tighten restrictions on the press, and curtail club and society gatherings to prevent political dissent. In December 1851, he would dissolve the National Assembly and stage a coup d'état that allowed him to write a new constitution instituting unlimited ten-year terms for a dictatorial president. A year later, he campaigned for a referendum that reestablished the French Empire. Music making continued in Paris throughout the uprisings and crises of government, as it always had, but individual musicians felt the effects of uncertainty and instability. All of the members of the Society for Classical Music except for Thérèse Wartel (its sole female member) had other permanent positions to shore up their income and to ensure that they could continue to play in such concerts even if audiences shrank and expenses ballooned in the volatile economic climate of Paris during the mid-century revolutions.

Although the Society for Classical Music had effectively disbanded by 1850, Farrenc's Nonet for winds and strings was clearly written with this group in mind. It addresses the group's mission to provide serious music to the Parisian public in a style that audiences accustomed to variety and novelty in their musical works would enjoy. Here and in her other chamber compositions, Farrenc demonstrates a clear and profound understanding of her colleagues and of their situation as presenters of music that fulfilled a distinct niche in Parisian concert life. By manipulating elements of form and texture to create something new, yet familiar, from earlier classical examples, she navigated the changing tastes of listeners to present them with a complex but inviting musical work. For the players themselves, she provided numerous opportunities to display the magnificent talents of expression and technical ability for which they had become justifiably famous. Chapter 2 explains how Farrenc's Nonet traverses a middle path that made this large ensemble work accessible and exciting for players and listeners alike.

Notes

1. "Il est question d'une soirée *par invitations*, qui sera donnée par Mme Farrenc, dans les salons de M. Erard, le mardi 19 courant." Emphasis in the original. [Anon.], "Nouvelles" *Revue et Gazette musicale de Paris* 17/9 (March 3, 1850): 75. All translations from French and German sources are my own, unless otherwise indicated.
2. "Nouvelles" *Revue et Gazette musicale de Paris* 17/9 (March 3, 1850): 75.
3. "Mme Farrenc a tenu le piano en véritable compositeur." Thérèse Wartel, "Nonetto de Mme Farrenc, exécuté pour la première fois dans la soirée donée le 19 mars." *Revue et Gazette musicale de Paris* 17/13 (March 31, 1850): 109.
4. "Et pour en revenir à la musique de chambre, qui est à la mode cette année, nous devons payer un juste tribut d'éloge à Mmes Farrenc et Wartel, ainsi qu'à Mlle Charlotte de Malleville, qui se sont livrées avec un brillant succès à ces charmantes conversations musicales, les deux dernières, en interprétant le savant *nonetto*, les quintettes, les trios de la première, sans préjudice de la belle musique de Mozart et de Beethoven." Henri Blanchard, "Auditions Musicales" *Revue et Gazette musicale de Paris* 17/13 (March 31, 1850): 109.
5. On historical constructions of women as ill-suited to intellectual activity (as both cause and result of their "natural" suitedness to domestic work), see Lynn Abrams, *The Making of Modern Woman: Europe, 1789–1918* (London: Routledge, 2002), especially chapter 1, "Body, Mind and Spirit"; and Charles Sowerwine, "Woman's Brain, Man's Brain: Feminism and Anthropology in Late Nineteenth-Century France" *Women's History Review* 12/2 (2003): 289–307.
6. Katharine Ellis, "Female Pianists and Their Male Critics in Nineteenth-Century Paris," *Journal of the American Musicological Society* 50/2–3 (1997): 353–385.
7. On the salon as a "liminal" space between the public and private spheres, see Rebecca Cypess, *Women and Musical Salons in the Enlightenment* (Chicago: University of Chicago Press, 2022).
8. On the perception of "seriousness" as a "German" quality among French musicians and critics, see Katharine Ellis, "The Limits of Seriousness: Piano Sonatas in 1840s Paris" in *Chopin's Musical*

Worlds: The 1840s, ed. Artur Szklener (Warsaw: Narodowy Instytut Fryderyka Chopina, 2007): 11–15.

9. Martin Wulfhorst, "Pierre Baillot: Against the Odds" *The Strad* 133/1582 (2022): 38–45; Joël-Marie Fauquet, "La Musique de chambre à Paris dans les années 1830" in *Music in Paris in the Eighteen-Thirties*, ed. Peter Bloom (Stuyvesant: Pendragon, 1987): 251–298.

10. Joël-Marie Fauquet, *Les Sociétés de musique de chambre à Paris de la restauration a 1870* (Paris: Amateurs de Livres, 1986).

11. Alexis Chitty, Maurice Brown, and Katharine Ellis, "Wartel family" in *Grove Music Online* 2023 https://doi.org/10.1093/gmo/9781561592630.article.29929.

12. Ibid.

13. "Nous renonçons à décrire l'effet de cette soirée: seulement constatons que "année 1845 marquera une nouvelle ère. – C'est l'avènement de la loi salique dans l'art du piano! – déjà un bataillon menace formidable la toute-puissance de la barbe : Mme Pleyel en tête puis la pianiste de la reine des Français, Mme Catherine de Dietz, Mlles Mattman, Bohrer, Farrenc, Masson, Joséphine Màrtia, Loveday, Wartel, etc., pléiade ravissant qui l'emportent, sans peine sur un sexe qui en général n'a rien de ravissant comme le confesse Franz Liszt lui-même dans sa fameuse dédicace. Nous ne croyons pas inutile ici de remettre sous les yeux de nos lecteurs cet étrange Morceau de littérature musicale: [Liszt's public dedication]" Anon., "Madane [sic] Pleyel" *Le Ménestrel* 12/18 (March 30, 1845): 2.

14. Ibid.

15. "Ce beau genre de mystique a remplacé la conversation française d'autrefois, que les femmes dirigeaient et dans laquelle elles étaient reines. Nous avons dit si souvent que Mme Wartel est un des organes les plus brillants de cette conversation, par la finesse et l'énergie de son jeu, par les temps intelligents qu'elle sait prendre, et qui prouvent qu'elle respire et ponctue d'un façon rationelle avec les doigts." Blanchard, "Auditions Musicales" *Revue et Gazette musicale de Paris* 17/13 (March 31, 1850): 109.

16. "La sonate a été dite par madame Wartel et M. Alard. Toutes ou pour ainsi dire toutes les pensées en ont été rendues avec précision, netteté et clarté. Madame Wartel n'a manqué ni de grâce ni de légèreté; mais, il faut bien le dire, nous avons désiré plus d'une fois cette mâle et chaleurese énergie litzéenne qui anime, qui vivifie tout. M. Alard, lui, a été expressif, passionné." [Anon.], "Concert de la Société Musicale" *Revue musicale, Journal des artistes, des amateurs et des théâtres* 6/05 (January 31, 1839): 43.

17. "Mad. Wartel ist eine Klavierspielerin, die eine sehr ansehnliche Fertigkeit besitzt und leichten graziösen Vortrage auf einer nicht gewöhnlichen Stufe steht; es fehlt ihrem Spiel nur dann und wann

etwas männliche Kraft, um ihren Leistungen einen wirklich bedeuten-
den Werth zu verleihen. Alle Stellen, wo dieses Plus, ihrer Natur nach,
nicht vermißt wird, gelingen ihr durchaus, und sie erwarb sich bei ihrem
neueichen ersten Auftreten die ungeteilte beifällige Anerkennung des
Publikums." Becher, "Concert von Herrn Fr. und Mad. Th. Wartel"
Allgemeine Wiener Musik-Zeitung II/137 (November 15, 1842): 550.

18. "Un concerto de Bach, une belle oeuvre de Beethoven, et le brillant
    morceau de salon de Weber lui ont offert l'occasion de montrer un
    talent sévère, solide et même masculin, sans que la force, l'éclat et la
    verve lui fassent oublier la grâce inhérente à sa qualité de jolie
    femme." Blanchard, "Coup d'oeil musical" *Revue et Gazette musi-
    cale de Paris* 11/13 (March 31, 1844): 117.

19. Thérèse Wartel, *Leçons Écrites sur les sonates pour piano seul de
    L. van Beethoven* (Paris: Girod, 1865).

20. Beate Angelika Kraus, "Elly Ney und Thérèse Wartel: Beethoven-
    Interpretation durch Pianistinnen – eine Selbstverständlichkeit?" In
    Der "männliche" und der "weibliche" Beethoven, ed. Cornelia
    Bartsch, Beatrix Borchard, and Rainer Cadenbach (Bonn: Beethoven-
    Haus, 2003): 445.

21. "Nachrichten" *Allgemeine musikalische Zeitung* 45/26 (June 28,
    1843): 472. The report is dated "Berlin, 2 June 1843."

22. The Paris correspondent for the *Allgemeine Wiener Music-Zeitung*
    reported on June 18, 1843, that the Wartels had returned to Paris after
    receiving "well deserved recognition" and that they "returned from
    their journey neither without fame nor without material advantages."
    (die beiden Künstler von ihrer Reise, weder ohne Ruhm, noch ohne
    materielle Vorteile zurückgekommen sind). *Allgemeine Wiener
    Music-Zeitung* 3/78 (July 1, 1843): 327. Thérèse seems to have
    arrived in Paris by June 25, 1843, but two separate reports in the
    Revue et Gazette musical de Paris suggest that François traveled
    alone from Dresden to St. Petersburg and Moscow, where he was
    engaged for the winter season. When Thérèse Wartel gave a concert
    at her brother-in-law's home in Paris the last week of March 1844,
    Henri Blanchard mentioned that she had been justly applauded with
    enthusiasm throughout Germany. Blanchard, *Revue et Gazette musi-
    cale de Paris* 11/3 (March 31, 1844): 117.

23. "Mme Wartel a exécuté sur le piano le concerto de salon par Weber,
    avec accompagnement de quatuor, de manière à se faire beaucoup et
    justement applaudir." [Anon.], "Coup d'œil Musical." *Revue et
    Gazette musicale de Paris* 11/16 (April 21, 1844): 139.

24. "La voici revenue cette exhibition de quatuors classiques, cette bonne
    musica da camera, ces séances qu'on a surnommées les soeurs de
    celles du Conservatoire si suivies et connues sous la dénomination de
    Société des concerts: là se retrouve le noyau des fidèles aux vais

principes de l'art; ce sont des artistes, des amateurs qui ne se laissent pas étourdir par le tohu-bohu, le dévergondage de la presse soi-disant musicale, qui forment le public de ces séances; et ce public n'applaudit jamais mal à propos, parce qu'il analyse ce qu'on lui donne." Blanchard, "Premier Concert de la Gazette musicale" *Revue et Gazette musicale de Paris* 11/52 (December 29, 1844): 435.

25. "Et d'abord, scientifiquement parlant, il commence par des harmonies étranges, par des accords aux résolutions les plus inattendues; ce serait presque du romantisme musical, si la régularité, l'unité de la pensée ne devaient témoigner aussitôt que ce n'est qu'un caprice momentané du génie." Ibid.

26. The phrase "pour violin et violoncelle" must be an error, as no such work by Mendelssohn survives, and no violinist is listed as playing with Cossmann in this program. The piece performed was probably Mendelssohn's second Cello Sonata, Op. 58, completed in June 1843 and first performed in Leipzig in November. Mendelssohn's other cello duos include the *Variations concertantes*, Op. 17 (publ. 1830), and the first Cello Sonata, Op. 45 (1839).

27. "Dans le culte qu'elle a voué à la musique classique et sévère, Mme Wartel, secondée par M. Cossmann, est venue nous dire le deuxième duo, pour violon et violoncelle, de Mendelssohn, morceau de science aride, beaucoup trop travaillé, et qui s'adressait avant tout aux contrapuntistes qui ne sont pas assez nombreux en France pour former un public. Quoi qu'il en soit, la jolie et habile pianiste nous a montré là, comme toujours, son exécution preste, accentuée, brillante et chaleureuse; mais on a mieux aimé retrouver ces qualités dans une étude de sa composition, et dédiée à Thalberg, qui n'était pas annoncée sur le programme, et qu'elle nous a dite en dédommagement du morceau par trop scolastique qu'elle avait exécuté avec M. Cossmann, l'un de nos meilleurs violoncellistes." Blanchard, "Premier Concert de la Gazette musicale" *Revue et Gazette musicale de Paris* 11/52 (December 29, 1844): 435. The Étude was probably No. 4 from Wartel's set of *Six Études de Salon*, published as her Op. 10 in 1850 and dedicated "à son maître F. HALÉVY, de l'Institute." See also Blanchard, "Impressions Des Autographes" *Revue et Gazette musicale de Paris* 11/45 (November 10, 1844): 345; and Blanchard, "Revue Critique" *Revue et Gazette musicale de Paris* 17/31 (August 4, 1850): 260–261.

28. *Letters from and to Joseph Joachim, Selected and Translated by Nora Bickley* (New York: Vienna House, 1972): 5–6.

29. "Für den nächstfolgenden Winter [1849–1850] wurde er wieder für die Gewandhausconcerte in Leipzig engagiert; doch blieb er hier nur drei Monate und ging dann mit Joachim nach Paris, um mit diesem Meister und der Pianistin Therese Wartet Soiréen für Kammermusik

bei Érard zu geben." Anon., "Biographisches: Bernhard Cossmann" *Musikalisches Wochenblatt* 2/49 (December 1, 1871): 773.

30. A letter survives from Louise Farrenc to an unnamed recipient asking them to play in a soirée to take place at her home in a few days; Farrenc apologizes for the short notice, saying that she is organizing some chamber music to include "Cossmann and a young violinist from Leipzig" in the hopes that they might help her get her orchestral music performed in Leipzig. Farrenc's biographer Bea Friedland proposes that the letter must have been written in February 1850 (Friedland, *Louise Farrenc*, 43–44 and 237, n.9). The programs for Wartel's concert series were announced on February 10 in the *Revue et Gazette musicale de Paris*, where the second concert was advertised as including Farrenc's Quintet in E for Piano and Strings.

31. In addition to the 1836 review of Farrenc's *Air russe varié* discussed in the Introduction, Robert Schumann reviewed Farrenc's works favorably in the *Neue Zeitschrift für Musik* 6/41 (May 23, 1837); 13/14 (August 15, 1840); and 15/30 (October 12, 1841). Farrenc also received critical acclaim in the musical press of Paris and Brussels.

32. Blanchard, "Silves musicales" *Revue et Gazette musicale de Paris* 12/27 (July 6, 1845): 221.

33. Joel-Marie Fauquet, *Les sociétés de musique de chamber à Paris de la Restauration à 1870*, 194. For the Society for Classical Music's programs, see pages 371–372.

34. "Les séances de musique de chambre données par madame Wartel et ses co-associés dans la salle Herz [. . .] ont toujours le privilège d'attirer bonne et nombreuse compagnie." *Revue et Gazette Musicale de Paris* 15/4 (January 23, 1848): 29.

35. "Sous le titre de *Société de musique classique*, douze artistes se sont réunis pour donner des concerts, qui seront pour la musique de chambre ce que eux de la célèbre Société, qui siège au Conservatoire, sont pour les chefs d'oeuvre symphoniques." "Nouvelles" *Revue et Gazette Musicale de Paris* 14/47 (November 21, 1847): 383.

36. Liszt, *Letters of Franz Liszt*, collected and edited by LaMara, translated by Bache (New York: Haskell House, 1968): 33–36.

37. "Ces deux ouvrages sont, comme ceux de M. Onslow, dans la manière de nos grands maîtres, avec les radieuses inspirations et le savoir sérieux qui caractérisent le talent de compositeur et de pianiste virtuose de cette artiste, licenciée ès-fugue et contrepoint. Elle a dit avec Dorus une sonate de Kuhlau pour piano et flûte, qui n'a fait que corroborer la haute estime qu'inspire ce compositeur, dont les ouvrages ne sont cependant pas très-connus en France." Blanchard, "Silves musicales" *Revue et Gazette musicale de Paris* 16/10 (March 11, 1849): 75.

38. "Mme Farrenc vient de terminer un nonnette pour instruments à cordes et à vent. Cette nouvelle compositions sera exécutée cet hiver par les premiers artistes de Paris." Notably, the report links this work to the success of Farrenc's symphonies in and beyond Paris: "Les symphonies de Mme Farrenc, et notamment celle qui a obtenu à la saison dernière un si beau succès au Conservatoire, seront entendues incessamment dans de brillants concerts qui se préparent." "Nouvelles," *Revue et Gazette musicale de Paris* 16/47 (November 25, 1849): 373.

39. On the March 19, 1850, public premiere, the Nonet was played by Dorus, the Verroust brothers, clarinetist Adolphe Leroy, Rousselot, Joachim, violist Adolphe Blanc, cellist Charles Lebouc, and Gouffé. Wartel, "Nonetto de Mme Farrenc" *Revue et Gazette musicale de Paris* 17/13 (March 31, 1850): 108–109.

40. "Nous avons en cette semaine l'occasion de l'entendre dans quelques salons, et nous pouvons affirmer que la renommée n'avait pas exagéré son mérite. M. Joachim n'est pas seulement un virtuose étonnant, qui, par exemple, exécute à lui tout seul une fugue à quatre parties de Bach; c'est un artiste dans l'acception la plus élevée de ce mot, qui interprète avec un sentiment profond les morceaux d'Ernst, les concertos de Beethoven, de Mendelssohn, les quatuors des grands maîtres, enfin tout ce qu'on peut appeler la grande et bonne musique." "Nouvelles," *Revue et Gazette musicale de Paris* 17/4 (January 27, 1850): 32.

41. On Joachim's position as a "learned virtuoso," see Karen Leistra-Jones, "Staging Authenticity: Joachim, Brahms and the Politics of Werktreue Performance" *Journal of the American Musicological Society* 66/2 (2013): 397–436; and idem., "(Re-)Enchanting Performance: Joachim and the Spirit of Beethoven" in *The Creative Worlds of Joseph Joachim* (Woodbridge: Boydell and Brewer, 2021): 86–103.

42. Katharina Uhde, "Joachim and Brahms in the Spring and Summer of 1853: Formative Influences and Performative Identities Reconsidered" in *Rethinking Brahms*, ed. Nicole Grimes and Reuben Phillips (Oxford: Oxford University Press, 2022): 174.

43. Elizabeth C. Bartlet, "Grand Opera (Fr.)" in *Oxford Music Online* 2001 https://doi.org/10.1093/gmo/9781561592630.article.11619. See also David Charlton (ed.), *Cambridge Companion to Grand Opera* (Cambridge: Cambridge University Press, 2003).

44. "Si le conflit de tant d'événements tumultueux entassés dans une seule année n'a pas entièrement dérouté la mémoire de nos lecteurs, ils sa souviendront sans doute qu'au début de la dernière saison musicale, de novembre 1847 à février 1848, il se manifesta à Paris une tendance sympathique, tout-à-fait inaccoutumée, en faveur de la musique instrumentale de chambre. Les sociétés qui se proposaient d'offrir

exclusivement à leurs abonnés des trios, des quatuors, des quintette, etc, surgirent en nombre notable, et, chose nouvelle, trouvèrent à qui parler.

Au plus fort de cette germination active, apparut pour la première fois la société dont le titre figure en tête de cet article. [...] Dès la première séance, datée du 28 novembre 1847, l'interêt le plus vif s'attacha à ces réunions, qu'un public tout spécial, un public de connaisseurs, couvrit de son patronage. Mais février ´clama comme la foudre. Réduite brusquement au silence par le formidable *tutti* des clameurs politiques, cette institution naissante dut s'effacer ainsi que bien d'autres, en attendant des jours meilleurs." Bourges, "Société de Musique Classique." *Revue et Gazette musicale de Paris* 16/6 (February 11, 1849): 44. Blanchard's review follows immediately, a rare, perhaps unique, case of both critics writing about the same event in a lengthy highlighted review for the same issue of the paper. Blanchard, "Auditions musicales" Ibid.: 45.

DIALOGUE AND PLAY IN THE NONET

As discussed in Chapter 1, Farrenc's Nonet for winds and strings was, if not explicitly composed for the Society for Classical Music, certainly inspired by it and the performing members of that group. The Society's stated aims and values, its *raison d'être*, echoed the artistic values that drove Farrenc in her activities as a performer, composer, and teacher, making it a natural ally in her own musical agenda, which had a two-pronged approach. First, following the models of her teacher and mentors (Anton Reicha, with whom she studied directly, and perhaps François-Joseph Fétis, who collaborated with her husband Aristide on music historical projects and took an active interest in Louise's compositions, performing and conducting them in Brussels as well as writing about them in the musical press), she sought to foster a greater appreciation of "serious" instrumental music based in the classical Viennese or German traditions among Paris's musical audiences and professional musicians. Second, she used her own familiarity with that repertoire and with emergent nineteenth-century harmonic, melodic, and formal techniques to produce innovative new musical works that combined the best of the old and the new styles. The Nonet, like Farrenc's other chamber works, "translates" the German style of serious music for French audiences, adding elements that would speak to their love of brilliant-style playing and dialogue within the framework of a four-movement sonata cycle. Capitalizing on the availability of diverse timbres within the nonet ensemble, Farrenc found new modes of expression that suited her innate love of variation and development. More than in earlier and contemporaneous examples by other composers, her Nonet uses the nine players as soloists most of the time and creates a constantly shifting array of new ensembles within the large group. Farrenc pointedly avoids both extremes evident in contemporaneous models: She neither treats the ensemble as a miniature orchestra, and thus avoids creating a petite symphony, nor allows a single player to dominate the texture as though the work was a chamber concerto. Rather, the nonet ensemble, though large, always effects an intimate chamber style that invites listeners to "eavesdrop" on overlapping conversations, as one might at a party at which friends gather together to catch up after a long hiatus. This insistence on dialogue and interaction reflects Farrenc's deep appreciation for the classical or serious style, an appreciation that she shared with the members of the Society for Classical Music.

Well-timed surprises, little moments of frisson or recognition, abound in Farrenc's work, creating an interactive experience for listeners as well, one that rewards attentive and repeated listening while also providing variety and novelty. By constantly inviting the listener to compare what they expected to hear – whether based on passages heard earlier in this work or based on familiarity with other works in the classical style – with what they are currently hearing, Farrenc involves the listener in the process of deciphering the music as it unfolds in performance. She achieves that interactive, playful element by continuously developing motivic ideas and phrases. Especially in the first and last movements, which are in two very different presentations of sonata form, Farrenc constantly shuffles elements from earlier themes like building blocks, repeating and sequencing ideas or reorchestrating motives to present them in new guises, breaking them down into smaller components, and then reassembling them in surprising ways. This motivic play, often carried out in dialogue among a small subset of players in the ensemble, gives the Nonet a vivacious, almost celebratory, atmosphere, even in its most learned passages. For listeners attuned to the compositional intricacies, the work provides a plethora of fine details to contemplate, and the analysis that follows in this chapter will catalog many of them. For listeners more interested in the theatrical elements of a work designed for nine virtuoso performers, these constant motivic rearrangements also provide many opportunities to enjoy the individual personalities on stage and for those players to show off their capabilities in brilliant-style passagework.

Understanding Form in Nineteenth-Century Music

This chapter primarily focuses on two aspects of the Nonet, both ultimately related to the idea of dialogue: texture, or the myriad ways that Farrenc varied the musical surface of the work to take advantage of virtuosic passagework and to create the impression of a conversation among friends within the ensemble, and form, which describes how she engaged the conventions of classical instrumental music and offered new approaches to familiar compositional processes. Both of these analytical priorities take cues from the writings of Farrenc's teacher Anton Reicha, whose treatises on composition circulated widely in the nineteenth century throughout Europe – they were translated into English and German and reprinted well into the later nineteenth century – and document aspects of his pedagogical approach that are evident in the works of his students. Although Reicha's principles are often based on examples from Haydn, Mozart, and their late-eighteenth-century contemporaries, his advice to students in the *Treatise on Melody* (1814) and *Treatise on Musical Composition* (1825–1826) also reflects changes in musical practice occurring in his lifetime, usually illustrated with musical examples of his composition.[1] This aspect of his treatises makes them especially useful for understanding how composers of the early nineteenth century expanded on the practices of Viennese Classicism in their development of a new Romantic sensibility in music. Using Reicha's understanding of instrumental form as a starting point allows modern scholars and listeners to take a historically informed stance to interpreting the music of Farrenc and her compatriots. (Simon P. Keefe has provided a useful introduction to Reicha's innovative explanations of musical dialogue in instrumental music, which serves as a model in some of the commentary that follows in this chapter.[2])

The analyses presented here take a dialogic approach to form, drawing on the philosophy of Warren Darcy and James Hepokoski's Sonata Theory.[3] This philosophy starts from the position that composers (and listeners) operate within a tradition of generic expectations based on the normative practices of their day that lend expressive weight to compositional choices

60

that fulfill or thwart those expectations. Rather than adopting wholesale the terminology of Sonata Theory, though, the chapter relies on the explanations of musical form provided by Reicha in his 1826 *Treatise on Musical Composition*. This treatment of form serves as a model with which Farrenc and her contemporaries would have been familiar and with which she entered into a creative dialogue in her works.[4] Reicha called the standard procedures of first-movement form in instrumental music the "grande coupe binaire" (large binary movement), which is equivalent to the form designated "sonata-allegro form" in some late twentieth-century analytical traditions or Sonata Theory's "Type 3" sonata, which is the most common form in the late eighteenth- and nineteenth-century repertoire. (Farrenc uses sonata form in the first and last movements of the Nonet, as she normally did in her instrumental works.) Reicha gave the reader a path through the typical form, famously illustrated with the first printed visual representation of musical form (see Figures 2.1 and 2.2). Many aspects of Reicha's description will be familiar to readers who

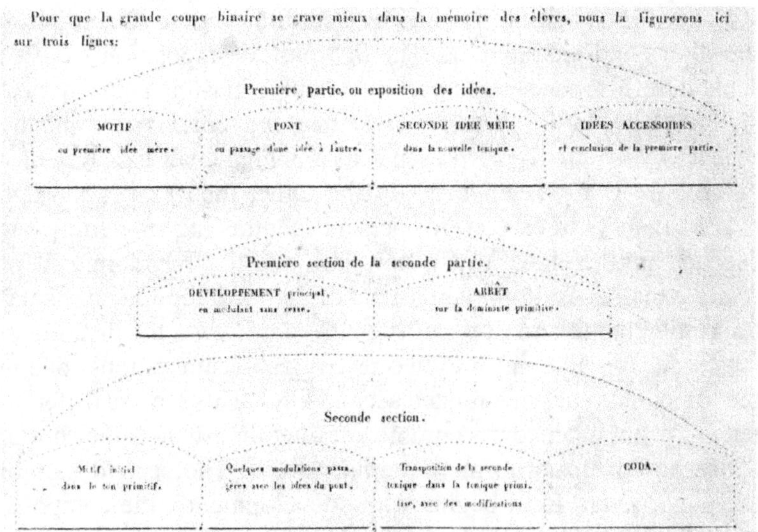

Figure 2.1 Visual aid showing the different parts of the "grande coupe binaire" (sonata form) from Anton Reicha, *Treatise on Musical Composition* (1826), p. 300.

First part, or exposition of the ideas.			
MOTIF or first mother idea	BRIDGE or passage from one idea to another	SECOND MOTHER IDEA in the new tonic	ACCESSORY IDEAS and conclusion of the first part

First section of the second part.	
Principal DEVELOPMENT, constantly modulating	STOP on the original dominant

Second section [of the second part].			
Initial Motif in the original key.	Some passing or temporary modulations with ideas from the bridge	Transposition of the second tonic in the original tonic, with modifications	CODA.

Figure 2.2 English translation of Reicha's visual aid.

have previously studied Classical music and its organizational conventions, but it will be helpful to summarize the relevant details here to clarify points of divergence from later descriptions.

Like earlier and contemporaneous writers, Reicha describes sonata form as a movement or piece in two large parts (i.e., a binary form) that are further divided into sections according to their keys and modulations. The first part, or exposition, is often separated from the second part by a double bar line and/or repeat sign and (except in overtures and finale movements) is typically repeated. The first part presents its opening material, Reicha's "motif, or first mother idea," in the tonic, then moves through a modulatory transition to present contrasting material (the "second mother idea") in a new key, usually the dominant or relative major. An important aspect of the form for all commentators active at the turn of the nineteenth century was the division of sonata form's first part into two recognizable subsections (one in the tonic, the other in a related second key). This feature differentiates it from other forms common at the time, such as the shorter dance-based binary forms or ternary form. The second part of a typical sonata form begins with "development"; the composer will vary, recompose, and combine motifs and ideas from the first part or introduce new ideas to be developed here. Reicha calls this section "the plot, or the crux" of the form.[5] This section ends in or

62

on the dominant of the original key: "After having offered the most interesting development, and after having traveled through a series of keys, we commonly stop on the original dominant, on which we often make a pedal followed by a transition to begin the following section."[6] (Some twentieth-century theories call Reicha's "stop" (*arrêt*) on the original dominant a "retransition" that prepares the return of the original key, while Sonata Theory refers to a "harmonically active dominant chord" and/or a "dominant lock." These terms all describe a suspenseful prolongation of dominant harmony, such as melodic figurations over a pedal point.) The second section of the second part presents materials heard in the first part (the exposition), now altered and transposed to the original key; modern sonata theories refer to this section as a "recapitulation." (I will use that familiar term because it is less clunky than "second section of the second part.") Saying relatively little about the reintroduction of earlier musical ideas, Reicha closes by saying that "we crown the piece with an interesting Coda,"[7] suggesting that he considered the coda a standard inclusion in the form, but not one with significant responsibility to close the musical processes of the work.

Several salient features of Reicha's description set it apart it from more familiar later theories and interpretations, and these offer important lenses through which to view early nineteenth-century French music like Farrenc's Nonet. First, Reicha's description does not characterize the relationship between the two themes or key areas of the exposition. Calling them simply first and second "mother ideas," he gives them no further differentiation or affective qualities. He describes the composition of a good musical idea at the beginning of this explanation of form and gives three examples of different ways to craft and extend a musical idea in order to have materials for later development. About the second theme, he says only, "This second motif is in [the dominant]. We can make the same remarks on it as on the initial motif, except that the repetition can also be done in [the minor dominant] when we wish to repeat it."[8] Later discussions of sonata form, on the other hand, refer to the second idea as "subordinate" or "secondary" and advise that this theme should present a strong contrast to the opening theme, often describing it as a more lyrical, softer, and more "feminine" theme. Adolf Bernhard Marx (1795–1866) famously characterized the subsidiary theme (*Seitensatz*) as

created after the first energetic confirmation and, by contrast, is that which serves. It is conditioned and determined by the preceding theme, and as such its essence is necessarily milder, its formation one of pliancy rather than pith – a feminine counterpart, as it were, to its masculine precedent. In just such a sense, each theme is a thing apart until both together form a higher, more perfected entity.[9]

This characterization, not especially noteworthy for readers at the time, but much repeated and expanded upon by later critics and writers on music, generated a great deal of scholarly critique in the 1990s, when feminist scholars began investigating the systemic biases of Western concert music traditions.[10]

The second major difference between Reicha's discussion of sonata form and that of his contemporaries is related to this apparent equalizing of the two thematic areas. Reicha's description places the greatest emphasis on the development and alteration of musical ideas or motives throughout the second part of the movement, not on the reconciliation or integration of disparate elements from the exposition or the reestablishment of the tonic in the recapitulation. As William O'Hara has recently noted, Reicha places the process of musical development at the center, or the "heart," of sonata form, emphasizing it above all other aspects and spending the most time in his treatises discussing how composers should develop their musical ideas.[11] A defining feature of sonata form for many later commentators, including Marx, is the return and alteration of the "secondary" or "subordinate" theme to fit into the primary theme's tonic and to (re)establish order and unity to the movement. Modern analysis typically treats this return as the attainment of a goal established at the outset of the movement. For example, Sonata Theory describes the recapitulation as "a structure of accomplishment: it fulfills the promise of the exposition," whose move away from the tonic had suggested "an eventual recovery and cadential affirmation of the tonic key."[12] Other analytical traditions, such as Donald Francis Tovey's *Essays in Musical Analysis* (1935–1939) or Charles Rosen's *The Classical Style* (1972) and Schenkerian analysis also emphasize organicism and unity or reconciliation in works that engage the Classical sonata form conventions.[13] This analytical emphasis was established in the mid-nineteenth century, above all, in the work of the aforementioned Marx. A staunch Romantic Idealist and disciple of Beethoven's music, Marx explained musical processes in terms of a Hegelian striving for unity and self-realization, generally using Beethoven's middle-period works as prime examples.[14] Late-nineteenth-century composers, critics, and theorists, strongly influenced by Romanticism themselves, took up similar aims in new musical works and in explanations of certain works that would form the nascent canon of classical music during the nineteenth century. But in the early nineteenth century, these ideals were not pervasive in treatises or in criticism of music, especially outside of the German-speaking world.

Reicha took a more agnostic approach to musical philosophy. He trained a generation of composers and performers with diverse interests and backgrounds over the course of several decades, including both private instruction and his work as a Professor of Counterpoint and Fugue at the Paris Conservatory beginning in 1818. His students would go on to very different careers and become representatives of a wide range of musical styles, from Farrenc and George Onslow to Hector Berlioz, Franz Liszt, Charles Gounod, and César Franck. Because Reicha's training was built on the construction of smaller units of melody and their development or extension, regardless of form or genre, it led students to apply his teachings in a wide variety of traditions and styles. Farrenc's tendency to constantly develop her musical materials throughout a movement, I propose, is an outgrowth of her studies with Reicha and of Parisian audiences's (and musicians's) love of variety and novelty.

That said, her innovative Romantic approach to composition – an extension of techniques she developed in her studies with Reicha as well as her individual studies and performance of contemporaneous works by Hummel, Moscheles, Chopin, and others – is clarified through a consideration of formal functions. This modern (late twentieth- and twenty-first-century) analytical approach focuses on the relationships between musical themes and components, especially as they connote temporal relationships or experiences of time in the unfolding of a musical work in performance. First expounded by William Caplin in relation to Viennese Classicism, recent scholarship has used this approach to interpret nineteenth-century composers' alterations of eighteenth-century procedures that play with listeners's and performers's expectations and to expand the expressive capabilities of concert music.[15] (I take as a model Anne Hyland's illuminating combination of Sonata Theory and Formal Functions in her analysis of Franz Schubert's chamber music.[16]) The analyses in this chapter occasionally make use of terminology and concepts from that analytical method to explain how Farrenc, an elder member of the Romantic generation who came of age in the 1820s–1830s (she was only six years older than Robert Schumann and Frederick Chopin, five years younger than Franz Schubert), enhanced and extended Classical genres and forms, modernizing them for Parisian audiences and musicians of the 1840s and beyond.

Movement 1: Adagio – Allegro

The Nonet's first movement is a perfect example of the development-focused approach to sonata form advocated by Reicha, and of Farrenc's careful balance between pleasurable surprises and structural clarity. It introduces the work and ensemble to listeners in an accessible style clearly built on the foundation of Viennese Classicism, but enlivened with more modern (Romantic) harmonic colorings and melodic lushness. Like examples by Farrenc's contemporaries and immediate predecessors, the melodic and harmonic writing in this movement privileges long lines and varied repetitions that provide multiple opportunities to add new shading and nuances to each musical idea. The work's focus on interaction between the winds and strings and on motivic play is evident already in the short Adagio section, which begins with full-ensemble chords but immediately moves to a legato melody in the clarinet and violin whose final flourish of sixteenth notes is repeated and passed around the ensemble. In the next two minutes of performance (just twenty-four measures of notated music), the ensemble runs through several different motivic ideas and textures, including an imitative descending scale in the winds,

66

a rising sixteenth-note line that passes from strings to winds and back, and a double-dotted fanfare motive in the strings that announces the arrival on the dominant near the end of the section. These constantly changing textures and the motivic variety of this opening establish the mood of the piece as exploratory and collaborative.

The sonata form movement that follows offers listeners many surprises and seeming musical detours in a fast-paced, vivacious atmosphere. (Table 2.1 provides an overview of the movement, mapped onto Reicha's visual plan for a standard sonata form.) Nineteenth-century listeners were unlikely to have a second opportunity to hear a work like this one, so the repeated exposition gave audiences a chance to rehear and reinterpret elements of the exposition and to catch details of the composition or its performance that might have gone unnoticed on first hearing. Given the open-ended thematic and harmonic design of the movement's two main themes, the first hearing of the exposition potentially raises many questions for listeners, as none of the themes in this part of the work follow a neat "beginning, middle, and end" design with clear cadential closes at the ends of phrases. Both the first musical idea in E flat and the second idea in B flat avoid a strong cadence in their respective tonics, which creates a palpable sense of expectation and forward motion in this movement, but also can lead to confusion about the relationships of particular motives to the overall form and harmonic trajectory. For modern listeners, the melodic and harmonic discursiveness of these themes may connect the Nonet (and Farrenc's compositional style generally) to the Romantic style of Schubert, whose long lyrical melodies and tendency to delay resolution into the dominant are hallmarks of an expanded conception of sonata form.[17] As musicologist Xavier Hascher has shown, Schubert's music first became known in Paris through his chamber works in the 1830s. Richault published French editions of the *Rondo brilliant* for violin and piano, Op. 70 (D895) in 1827, the Piano Trio in E flat (D929) in 1829, and two string quartets (D87 and D353) in 1831. Hascher documents performances of the piano trio at a matinée held by the Tilmant brothers (who collaborated with Farrenc on many occasions and intended to perform at the

Table 2.1 *Overview of sonata form in Farrenc Nonet, movement 1 (Allegro).*

First part or exposition of ideas	*First motive, or "mother idea"*	*Bridge, or passage from one idea to another*	*Second mother idea in the new tonic*	*Accessory ideas and conclusion of the first part*
	mm. 24–45	mm. 46–84	mm. 85–122	mm. 123–164
	Open-ended theme, moving from E flat to B flat (I to V7)	Fanfare gesture in E flat, moving to B flat; then motivic dialogue, ending with an F pedal	Open-ended theme moving B flat to F7, ending with a "purple patch" followed by a cadence onto F	Three discrete closing themes, all in B flat major
First section of the second part	*Principal Development, constantly modulating*			*Stop on the original dominant*
	mm. 169–223			mm. 224–231
	New theme in D major; variant of first motive in F major; then A flat and G major alternation			Brief pedal point on the dominant
Second section of the second part	*Initial motive in the original key*	*Some temporary/passing modulations with ideas from the bridge*	*Transposition of the second key in the original key, with modifications*	
	mm. 232–253	mm. 254–292	mm. 293–330	mm. 331–385
		Fanfare gesture in E flat, moving to B flat; the pedal section removed	open-ended theme in E flat, ending on B flat 7, followed by a "purple patch" and cadence onto B flat	Three discrete closing themes, all in E flat

Table 2.1 (*cont.*)

Coda	mm. 371–385	386–417
	Transition and prolongation of predominant harmony, ending with a cadenza for the violin	First motive or mother idea played by the horn in E flat, then passed around the ensemble; closing with high fast passage-work for violin before cadence in E flat

private premiere of the Nonet in 1849) during the 1833–1834 season. The Tilmants played several other chamber works by Schubert later in the 1830s.[18] In Farrenc's Nonet, as in Schubert's chamber music, these diversions into surprising harmonic regions and the spinning-out of thematic motives also provide opportunities to vary timbre and texture, in this case, making the best use of the expanded instrumental palette provided by an ensemble of nine solo wind and string players.

The movement proper begins at m. 24 with an asymmetrical first mother idea (see Ex. 2.1; all musical examples in this volume use concert pitch throughout to make the analysis accessible to the greatest number of readers). The opening eight-bar phrase played by the violin with supporting harmonies in the lower strings and horn seems at first to prepare a balanced contrasting period, but the second half of the phrase, which prolongs a B flat harmony, does not resolve onto the tonic as one might expect, based on conventional thematic construction in the Classical style. Instead, a sudden tonicization of C minor (vi) in m. 31 avoids cadential closure and launches the musical texture into a roving melodic sequence in mm. 32–46, based on a new motive whose rising second measure gives it the quality of a beginning gesture, rather than a closing one. The rising arpeggio and its accompaniment create an authentic cadence (B flat 7 to E flat, or V7–I), but the motive stops just before attaining the downbeat, giving it an unfinished effect that begs for an answer and/or continuation. Hence, as the motive bounces from one instrument to another in the ensemble, the sequence cycles through E flat to F to A flat, then C flat (flat VI) before pausing on

Example 2.1 Farrenc Nonet, movement 1, mm. 24–45 (first mother idea).

a cadential 6/4 chord and cadencing firmly in the tonic at m. 46. This twenty-two-measure opening passage establishes a mood of playful interaction among the ensemble members that will dominate the work, but it also sets up a process of continual elaboration and suspended anticipation that creates dramatic flair. As in the extended cadences of Rossini and other opera composers (Donizetti, Bellini, Spontini), who were popular with Parisian theater audiences in the first half of the nineteenth century, these sequential passages increase the sense of anticipation for the eventual close onto the tonic. Farrenc draws out the theme here to highlight the unique timbre of each individual instrument before bringing them together into a climactic *forte* fanfare (mm. 46–54) that harkens back to the opening call to attention from the first measures of the work. Notably, this use of motivic imitation and variation also exemplifies Reicha's definition of musical dialogue, including the expectation that all the voices will unite at the end of the passage.[19]

The contrast of this relatively "loose," exploratory first theme with the rigid, reiterated progression in the tonic represented by the fanfare reverses the expected characters of these two formal sections. The fanfare takes the place of a transitional bridge, a role that is clarified when a variation of it is played in mm. 54–61. This soft version in the winds closes with a cadence in B flat, effecting the transition from first key to second key in just four measures. Although the materials that follow have a more transitional (looser) melodic style based on motivic dialogue, the passage from mm. 62 to 84 serves mostly as a confirmation of the new key with movement from B flat to F and back.

The movement's second mother idea follows a narrative arc very much like the first theme, in that it begins with a predictable antecedent phrase, but then splinters into several distinct motivic exchanges as different instruments pick up elements and pass them back and forth in a modulatory style, rather than presenting a rounded theme with an audible beginning, middle, and end in a clearly articulated second key. (In other words, it, too, functions more like a transitional or developmental passage than a traditional "secondary" or lyrical theme.) The violin takes center stage at the beginning of this section, as it presents the opening eight-measure phrase in mm. 85–92, accompanied by the cello. The phrase ends with an inconclusive half-cadence onto F major (V of B flat), rather than a strong arrival on the new tonic. Then the violin and lower strings exchange a two-measure motive that suggests a sequence will follow, but the accompanying passagework in the winds takes over the texture and leads the ensemble on a series of harmonic adventures before finally cadencing on B flat in m. 123.

Already in these expositional passages, Farrenc demonstrates a development-focused compositional technique that uses instrumental dialogue to explore motivic features and prolong melodic gestures to create a typically Romantic, expansive style. A characteristic feature of Farrenc's harmonic and formal language, one that links her to other early Romantic figures like Schubert, is the "purple patch," a term coined by early twentieth-century writer Donald F. Tovey to describe a harmonically surprising musical passage that averts cadential resolution and thereby delays the music's arrival at its harmonic goal.[20] The implied comparison to "purple prose" suggests that such passages interrupt the music's forward momentum and revel in an extravagant or flamboyant diversion, but this characterization assumes a linear, goal-directed sonata form philosophy that, as noted earlier in this chapter, is more in keeping with a Hegelian musical ideal (articulated by A. B. Marx and perpetuated by later writers) than the exploratory style described in Reicha's treatises. In the music of Farrenc and many of her contemporaries, these colorful detours enliven the musical surface and offer further opportunities for development and motivic play. In the Nonet's first movement exposition, for example, the passage at mm. 109–118 veers suddenly toward E major, delaying resolution into B flat for ten measures and allowing the ensemble to develop thematic ideas from the second mother idea (see Ex. 2.2). Here, the music has effectively prepared a strong authentic cadence with movement from an E diminished chord through B flat to F major (vii° of V, I6/4, V7), but on the downbeat of m. 109, an unexpected F sharp diminished harmony leads into E (natural) major and presents the beginning of an alternate theme before modulating back to B flat. This colorful parenthesis in the middle of an otherwise mundane authentic cadence dramatically thwarts listener expectations by inserting harmonic instability when it is least expected; it elongates the thematic idea and energizes the cadence by delaying and drawing out the resolution to the new tonic.

After having definitively confirmed the modulation to B flat major with a strong cadence in that key at m. 123, the music presents a long closing section (Reicha's "accessory ideas and conclusion to

Example 2.2 Farrenc Nonet, movement 1, mm. 107–120 ("purple patch" in exposition).

the first section") that repeatedly cadences in the new tonic. At forty-three measures in length, it is the longest stretch of music with a clear and continuous formal function heard so far, and the repeated cadences and arpeggiations of tonic harmony act as assurances that the music has found its harmonic destination. Three distinct sub-sections highlight different families within the ensemble in increasingly showy passagework that drives this section to a satisfying close. First the strings play an arch-shaped arpeggiated motive, passed between the violin and cello and supported with subdued chords in the lower winds (mm. 123–136); the head motive's decorative trill makes the closing theme memorable, which will aid its effectiveness as a signal of closure when it returns at the end of the movement. The second sub-section (mm. 137–148) flips the roles of the two instrument families by giving the arpeggiated motive to the clarinet and bassoon while the strings provide support with the same chordal pattern heard earlier in the winds.

73

When this passage cadences onto B flat major at m. 148, the third sub-section introduces a new musical idea in triplet rhythms. This final subsection closes with a forte triplet passage that brings the ensemble together in a rousing repeated B-flat major chord. (The first ending adds an A flat to this sonority, instantly transforming the new tonic back into its original dominant-seventh function, which will lead smoothly to the opening of the exposition.)

The short development section (mm. 175–231) extends and builds upon the harmonic adventurousness on display elsewhere in the work. At a structural level, the tonal centers visited in the development follow a chain of thirds from the dominant (B flat) at the exposition's close to D major at the beginning of the development proper, then F major and finally A flat major, arpeggiating the dominant seventh chord. On a more local level, the modulation to D major in the second ending of the exposition (which serves as a transition to the development section) is especially striking. Rather than construct a smooth transition that gradually leads the listener from B flat to its mediant, Farrenc employs an unexpected half-step motion in the bass that wrenches the harmony from the flat side of the scale into sharps at m. 165 (see Ex. 2.3). The exposition's codetta had ended with a strong cadence in B flat and an extension of this harmony in mm. 161–164. When the players take the second ending, though, this B flat shifts up unexpectedly to B natural in the bass voices (double bass, cello, and bassoon) while the topmost voice (flute) rises from F to A flat, resulting in a B (natural) diminished seventh chord. The next five measures move through C minor and C sharp diminished harmonies to land on an A dominant seventh chord in m. 174 (the passing B flat in the violin's arpeggio suggests a ninth chord), that resolves at the bar line onto the new tonic D major. The notated key change and double bar line indicate the beginning of the development section here in m. 175, where a new theme also highlights the beginning of the new section and characterizes the key. The development theme combines a new legato phrase first presented by the violin against a familiar triplet motif in the flute, then the clarinet – this motif had provided a lively reiteration of B flat in the final measures of the codetta, giving that key stability as the new tonic. Here the triplet motif gives Farrenc a memorable melodic passage to sequence as it

74

Example 2.3 Farrenc Nonet, movement 1, mm. 160–192 (exposition second ending and new development theme).

passes around the ensemble, cascading from D through B and E major to rest briefly on A minor (v in the local tonic) before articulating a C dominant seventh chord in mm. 187–88. Thus, the new theme is treated much the same way that the exposition themes had been, as an open-ended launchpad for further modulations.

Example 2.3 (cont.)

The second portion of Farrenc's development moves to F major, clearly marked with another key change in the score, and presents a new version of the movement's first mother idea, played by the woodwinds over rolling eighth-note passagework in the cello. Unlike the exposition's version of this theme, though, here the first eight measures close with an authentic cadence in the local tonic (F, in m. 196) before beginning a modulation away from that key in the following measure. Thus, in the development section, the theme is more "closed" and stable than its open-ended counterpart in the exposition. The cello line's perpetual motion continues in the subsequent section with shorter patterns and a rising pitch level on each downbeat. These changes to the cello part increase the harmonic and timbral tension as the music climbs into the high range of the instrument, and the woodwind parts add a disruptive rhythmic element with a syncopated rising line and a gradual crescendo in the oboe to further increase the anticipation for a resolution at the end of the passage. This modulatory action and rhythmic complexity settle down in mm. 204–207, when the music pauses on A flat, the final waystation on the development's harmonic path. The final portion of the development lacks identifiable themes or motives, but creates a shimmering play of ensemble textures over pedal tones. Alternating between A flat major and G major, this final section (mm. 205–223) teeters between the flat side and sharp side of the tonal spectrum. In the harmonic context of the movement as a whole, G major represents V of vi, the conventional endpoint, or "point of furthest remove" for modulatory development sections in the Viennese Classical style that formed the basis for Farrenc's training.[21] Farrenc enlivens the distant tonal destination with a half-step ornamentation that also provides a common tone for the shift back to the dominant of E flat major (the work's tonic).

Whereas the movement up to this point has been filled with unprepared half-step modulations, the move in mm. 220–224 from G major to B flat, the point where the movement stops on the dominant (Reicha's "arrêt" and later theorists's "retransition"), is smooth, marked with a gentle falling arpeggiated motive passed from the flute to the viola to the bassoon. The seeming inevitability of this motive's gentle descent through the dominant chord leads the listener home to the tonic at m. 228, where the double bass takes over for the first time in the work with a slow trill and a rising scale that arrives triumphantly on E flat at the downbeat of m. 232. The initial motive, or mother idea, returns in the original key here, signaling the beginning of the recapitulation.

Farrenc's recapitulation in this first movement adheres to the established pattern of the exposition with few melodic alterations. The proportions of the recapitulation are the same as those of the exposition, with melodic materials and motifs transposed to the tonic as Reicha indicates. Farrenc's re-orchestration of these materials, though, provides a wealth of interest and nuance based in a timbral exploration of the ensemble and its abilities, and in some cases, the instrumentation changes alter the affect (the apparent formal function) of particular passages. For example, the bridge between the first and second key areas in the exposition used a two-measure staccato motif passed from one instrument to another to facilitate a modulation from the tonic to the dominant, working towards tonicization of B flat major with an F pedal in the horn part in mm. 72–80. In the recapitulation, this passage is altered by placing the staccato arpeggio and scale motive in a single voice (in the flute for mm. 272–279, answered with a complementary passage in the violin in mm. 280–283), while the other voices provide legato support. Whereas the earlier passage changed pitch in each iteration as it passed around the ensemble to facilitate the modulation, here the continuous line establishes E flat minor, which provides additional color and variety to this brief transition section, then closes with a half-cadence on a B flat sonority in m. 288. A five-measure violin solo leads cleanly to the recapitulation of the second theme in the tonic major. Earlier, in the exposition, chopping the theme into two-measure motives passed around the ensemble created an exciting conversational texture that suggested movement, vivacity, and constant change, but here the continuity created by placing the entire melodic line in one instrument uses texture to create stability and consistency for listeners. Here and throughout the Nonet, Farrenc harnesses timbre and texture to augment the effect of harmonic formal functions. In this instance, they enhance the stability of the tonic minor as an intermediary harmonic space that offers contrast between the movement's two main themes stated in the same key in this recomposed transition.

Farrenc's expert writing for individual instruments and instrumentalists is on display throughout the Nonet, but the first movement contains several special gestures that shine a spotlight on the violin in particular as the leader of the ensemble. The exposition includes a notated cadenza at the end of the recapitulation, in addition to brief transitional solo passages that lead the ensemble and the listener into new thematic areas (see mm. 80–84 in the exposition, mm. 288–292 in the recapitulation). These solo opportunities may be heard as special concessions to Parisian audiences accustomed to virtuosic display in newly composed instrumental works. Yet, the cadenza itself shows considerable restraint, which may be a reason why Farrenc's music appealed to Joseph Joachim when it was introduced to him, as suggested in Chapter 1. Shown in Example 2.4, the cadenza does not employ extraordinary technical display – the classically oriented style of the figuration is well within the traditions of the French Violin School typified by Giovanni Battista Viotti, Pierre Rode, and Pierre Baillot. Although it is certainly possible that Joachim or another violinist might improvise or compose a more virtuosic cadenza, Farrenc's manuscript clearly communicates her intentions for a modest, but highlighted opportunity for the soloist to display their sensitive touch, phrasing, and musical timing, rather than the left-hand acrobatics or bow-arm shenanigans involved in the double-stops, harmonics, and bariolage that frequently appeared in concerto cadenzas of the day. In other words, the cadenza and other soloist passages peppered throughout the Nonet reflect a chamber music aesthetic of refined elegance and sensitivity to the equality of the ensemble.

In this way, Farrenc's Nonet departs from the "brilliant" or "concertante" style of popular chamber showpieces by virtuoso violinists like Louis Spohr, Baillot, and Pierre Rode and pianists like Hummel and Johann Peter Pixis. These and other virtuoso performer-composer personalities had capitalized on a popular style of chamber work that functioned like a chamber concerto, i.e., that highlighted one or (less often) two soloists while the remainder of the ensemble accompanied them. The term "concertante" comes from the *symphonie concertante*, a genre for multiple soloists and orchestra that was especially popular in Paris in the late eighteenth and early nineteenth centuries.[22] (Although most of this repertoire fell out of favor in the later nineteenth century, Mozart's Sinfonia concertante for violin, viola, and orchestra, K. 364, continued to be played regularly and therefore has become the most familiar example that

Example 2.4 Farrenc Nonet, movement 1, mm. 381–391 (violin cadenza and beginning of Coda).

persists in the modern repertoire. The long legacy of the *sinfonie concertante* is evident, though, in later works like Beethoven's 1803 Triple Concerto for piano, violin, and cello and Brahms's Double Concerto for violin and cello, composed in 1887.) In chamber music, eighteenth-century "concertante" works featured an alternation of solos or soloistic playing accompanied by the rest of the ensemble, giving each member of the group an opportunity to demonstrate their skill and to shine in lyrical themes and/or technical display.[23] They, too, were unusually popular in Paris in the last decades of the eighteenth century, though some German cities like Mannheim, which had a famously talented and well organized court orchestra filled with virtuoso wind and string players, also supported the genre. Around 1800, the concertante quartet became overshadowed by the *quatuor brillant*, or the "brilliant-style" quartet, in which one instrument, usually the first violin, is treated as a soloist playing technically demanding parts lightly accompanied by their colleagues. This style of chamber work remained popular in Paris well after it had fallen out of favor elsewhere in Europe, lending credence to the perception among nineteenth-century critics and musicians that Paris valued virtuosic display or technical proficiency rather than compositional "depth" or seriousness, which continued to be associated with the Viennese (or "German") tradition of complex motivic work and polyphonic textures.[24]

In the Nonet, though, the violin's cadenza even goes a step further in collegiality, and thereby distances the work and the performer from contemporaneous brilliant-style traditions, as it charmingly leads into the coda and a statement of the work's primary theme by the French horn. The horn had played an important supportive role up to this point in the work and had several opportunities to trade motivic material in dialogue with other instruments, but until this moment, late in the movement, it had not received a spotlighted solo. This statement of the primary theme places the horn at the forefront of the texture, with just the violin and cello accompanying at first. Even after the other instruments enter the texture and take over motives from the theme, the horn retains its role as soloist with a showy passage of arpeggiated eighth notes that require outstanding stamina and technique to play at the fast tempo, especially on the natural horn that was in use during the late 1840s. Here as elsewhere in the work, Farrenc demonstrates careful awareness of the instruments in her ensemble and the best ways to make them shine, and she provides opportunities for each player to act as soloist, highlighting the musicality and virtuosity of her colleagues from the Conservatoire and her friends from Paris's musical community.

Movement 2: Andante con moto

The Nonet's second movement is a Classically oriented set of five variations on an original theme, which follows the model of several popular works for large mixed ensemble that were played often in Paris during the 1840s. Both Beethoven's Septet for Winds and Strings, Op. 20, and Hummel's Septet for Piano, Winds, and Strings, Op. 74, included Andante variation movements, as did the Nonets by Onslow and Spohr that the Society for Classical Music had performed in their 1848 and 1849 seasons. Farrenc's movement follows the conventions of this form evident in these models and in Reicha's description of the variations movement in his composition treatise (where he notes Haydn as an important model[25]), demonstrating awareness of the tradition while also, perhaps, inviting comparison with popular examples. Farrenc had composed many free-standing sets of variations for solo piano and for piano with orchestral accompaniment in the 1820s and 1830s, but this movement and the middle movement in her Op. 34 piano trio are the only variation sets within multi-movement works. They differ significantly from the showpieces of her earlier output. Whereas the free-standing variation sets generally engage in the dramatic virtuoso style of the day using themes from popular operas like Onslow's *Colporteur*, Donizetti's *Anna Bolena*, and Meyerbeer's *Les Huguenots* as jumping-off points, here and in the piano trio's second movement, Farrenc composed her own tune as the basis for a set of five more restrained and melodically diverse variations. Like other variation sets within chamber works of the time, Farrenc includes a minor-mode variation as the penultimate portion of the movement, followed by an up-tempo "finale" (Variation 6, an "Allegretto" in 6/8 time) that provides a welcome contrast to the theme and its previous iterations. This practice aligns well with Reicha's advice to include an episode to give the listener a break from the theme and to introduce novelty in the work.

The Nonet's Andante movement begins with a simple sixteen-measure binary theme that bears some striking similarities to the theme of Beethoven's Andante ("Thema con variazioni") from the fourth movement of his Septet in the same key (see Ex. 2.5a and 2.5b). Both themes use a stately, measured rhythm in eighth notes with staccato separations that give the theme a light, graceful air. They both give the strong impression of a stylized contredanse, an English social dance that reached peak popularity on the European

Example 2.5a Beethoven Septet, movement 4, mm. 1–16 (main theme).

continent in the late eighteenth century and showed up in numerous instrumental works and operas during that era. They both divide neatly into four-measure phrases. The symmetrical binary structure of the themes as two repeated eight-measure periods gives each composer a clear, predictable structure to follow in subsequent variations, and both composers retain this sixteen-measure model for most of their variations, including the tonal and cadential structure with a strong articulation of phrase endings at m. 4 and m. 12. (See Table 2.2 for an overview of the form in Farrenc's Andante movement.) Beethoven's theme is a simple rounded binary form: mm. 1–4 state an antecedent phrase that closes with a half cadence on V, answered by a consequent phrase (mm. 5–8) that closes with an imperfect cadence in the tonic; after the repeat sign, a contrasting phrase is presented in mm. 9–12, bringing the music to V of V before familiar motivic material (an

Example 2.5b Farrenc Nonet, movement 2, mm. 1–16 (main theme).

altered version of mm. 5–8) returns to close the theme with a perfect authentic cadence in the tonic.

Farrenc's theme expands on this Classical design in three important ways, opening up opportunities for greater musical drama later in the movement. First, the structure of her theme as a more continuous sixteen-measure binary form with a half cadence onto F major (V) at m. 8 gives her theme a stronger sense of tension and resolution, providing motion away from the tonic and a return "home" that she uses to good advantage in the variations. The harmonic narrative of the theme, with its tonicization of F in the middle and accented G minor chord (vi, highlighted with a secondary dominant at mm. 12–13) at the beginning of the final phrase gives the theme greater variety and opportunities for further exploration of related keys, while maintaining a clear sense of direction and purposeful movement toward resolution. Second,

Movement 2: Andante con moto

Table 2.2 *Overview of variations form in Farrenc Nonet, movement 2 (Andante).*

Theme	‖: mm. 1–8 :‖	‖: 9–12	13–16 :‖	
Andante con moto 2/4 time	Strings only, B flat major, ending on F (V)	Winds only, F major	All, full texture; D (V of vi) moving to B flat major (I)	
Var. 1	‖: mm. 17–24 :‖	‖: 25–32 :‖		
	Oboe melody, accompanied by strings	Dialogue: Oboe, viola, cello		
Var. 2	‖: mm. 33–40 :‖	‖: 41–44	45–48 :‖	
	Dialogue: violin and viola	Clarinet, Flute, Bassoon; Violin		
Var. 3	‖: mm. 49–56 :‖	‖: 57–60	61–64 :‖	
	Winds only, new countermelody	Winds continued;	winds and strings	
Var. 4	‖: mm. 65–72/73 :‖	‖: 74–77	78–81	82–88 :‖
	Horn and violin (triplets in violin); B flat minor, ending on F minor	Full texture Horn, strings F to G flat (flat VI) to B flat minor		flute triplets; D flat (flat III) to F major
[Var. 5]	mm. 89–96	‖: 97–104 :‖		
Allegretto 6/8 time	Imitation in strings, B flat, ending on F (V)	Duos: Oboe and clarinet, Violin and Viola F to B flat (I)		
[Coda]	105–112	113–120		121–128 ‖
	Double bass lead-in, then full texture; B flat major	Winds only, B flat major		Strings, flute, and oboe B flat major

the minimal repetition of motives or subphrases in her theme provides many distinct motives for variation and recombination, while the decorative melodic flourishes at the cadential points (the sixteenth-note figures in mm. 7 and 15, the grupetto in m. 4) provide consistency and finality at those resting points in the melody.

Third, Farrenc's scoring of the theme makes good use of the modern instruments at her disposal, and the play of different textures establishes the winds and strings as equal partners, as opposed to Beethoven's emphasis on the stringed instruments. Farrenc's first eight-measure phrase is played by the strings in a homophonic texture, with the violin playing the melody to accompaniment from the other three players. But the second period begins with a strongly contrasting polyphonic idea in the winds; the oboe and clarinet play a melody in parallel thirds, joined first by the bassoon and then the horn in independent imitative lines. When the strings join the ensemble for the final four-measure phrase, the full group moves together in a shared eighth-note rhythm (i.e., in a homophonic, homorhythmic texture) through a colorful harmonic progression that leads from the dissonant V of vi through C minor (ii) to the cadence in B flat at mm. 15–16. This theme displays the inherent differences between the two mini ensembles within the nonet: The strings blend together into a unified sound due to their similar timbre, and they function here as a single unit, but the winds each have a distinctive tone color, making a blended sound impossible and undesirable. Rather than attempt to play as a unified entity here, each voice enters the texture individually, highlighting their unique tone and creating a dynamic and timbral crescendo in mm. 13–16 as the texture fills to full capacity at the height of the cadence. By contrast, in Beethoven's theme, the string instruments introduce the opening phrase and are then joined by the winds for a full ensemble repetition; the second half of the theme is played by the full ensemble with the strings in a leading role. This scoring of the theme foreshadows the roles of the different instruments that will follow in Beethoven's variations. The movement highlights different combinations of strings (viola-violin duo, violin-viola-cello trio), and the violin alone enjoys opportunities to display a brilliant performance style, with runs of thirty-second notes in a high range in Variation 2, for example, and triplet figurations in Variation 4. Variation 3 is the only one that features the winds as soloists, with a duet version of the theme's first phrase played by the clarinet and bassoon. Thus, while Beethoven's work exemplifies the style of his day and the abilities of the performers and instruments available to him, Farrenc's Nonet demonstrates the advances in instrumental design and playing (not to mention harmonic language) that had occurred in the half-century since Beethoven composed his Septet.

Farrenc's technique builds on the dramatic instrumentation of her theme, as she highlights different smaller ensembles within the nonet in each variation. In this way, she avoids a potentially tedious tour of the ensemble in which each player might present a solo variation, which would also lead to an overly long slow movement, while also sidestepping the tendency to treat the ensemble as a miniature orchestra. (As, for example, both Spohr and Onslow's Nonets tend to do, including in their variation movements, by utilizing the ensemble as a more unified body of sound. Both composers tend to write for the nonet in three- or four-part textures with various instruments doubling each other in families, often treating the strings as members of a supporting ensemble against the winds, instead of as four individual voices, or having the low instruments double each others' parts to reinforce a strong bassline more often than giving them distinct or soloistic roles in the ensemble.) Farrenc's Andante rarely uses the full nine-instrument ensemble, which is reserved for dramatic effect until Variation 4. Variations 1 and 2 emphasize soloistic playing in the first half of the theme and ensemble work in the second half. The unusual timbre of the viola and oboe duet in mm. 25–28 demonstrates Farrenc's gift for charming instrumentation, and the carry-over of the viola as a soloist answering the violin's passagework in the next variation provides continuity while giving the violist (Paris's much-in-demand chamber violist Casimir Ney in early performances) further opportunities to demonstrate their prowess. The clarinet, flute, and bassoon engage in a playful exchange of arpeggios in the second half of Variation 2. In Variation 3, in which the string instruments play only in the final four-measure phrase, the bassoon presents the main theme while the oboe and clarinet introduce a new counter-melody based on the rhythmic motive that characterized the first cadence in the theme (m. 4).

The most interesting portion of the movement, from the standpoint of dialogue with previous models, is Variation 4, which shows a striking similarity to the fourth section of Beethoven's

Example 2.6a Beethoven Septet, movement 4, mm. 81–88 (Variation 4, first half).

Op. 20 while also departing from the strict formal procedures of the earlier variations in a way that suggests the influence of Hummel's popular Septet for Piano, Winds, and Strings, Op. 74. As Beethoven did in his Septet, Farrenc placed her fourth variation in B flat minor. Both iterations begin with triplet passagework for the violinist, accompanied by the horn (see Ex. 2.6a and 2.6b). Beethoven's newly composed horn line provides harmonic support for the violin's presentation of the theme, whose ornamented melodic structure follows the general shape of the original theme within a slightly altered harmonic framework. (The minor-mode variant replaces some dominant chords with subdominants, creating a more continuous melodic style than the square alternations of the tonic and the dominant that establish the key in the original theme.) When the horn theme is taken up by the clarinet and bassoon playing in octaves in the second half of the phrase, the viola joins the violin in octaves as well,

Example 2.6b Farrenc Nonet, movement 2, mm. 65–73 (Variation 4, first half).

providing the fuller ensemble sound familiar from the scoring of the theme and previous variations.

Farrenc's scoring of triplet figuration in the violin with a legato melody in the horn recalls Beethoven, but her variation places the original theme in the horn part, giving that player a rare chance to enjoy the spotlight in this variation. The violin's accompanying triplet pattern provides a ripple in the otherwise placid texture of the variation. The introduction of a rhythmic pattern that we have not heard yet in this movement offers novelty, energizing the passage, and its emphasis on G flat (flat $\hat{6}$) highlights the harmonic shift to the minor mode, creating an ominous atmosphere in sharp contrast with the rest of the movement. The horn takes up the triplet motif in the second phrase, animating its F pedal as the music modulates to the minor dominant. The second half of the variation continues to highlight the horn in vivacious rhythmic motives that demonstrate the instrument's range and allow it to step out of the role of bass-voiced accompaniment. Throughout this variation, the violin and other instruments play a supporting role: Technically brilliant and in a playful dialogue with other members of the ensemble, they dance around the horn's melody and interact with it rather than overshadowing its presentation of the theme.

For the first time in the movement, Farrenc extends the thematic structure at the end of this variation, adding an eight-measure transition after the second ending's cadence. Prior to this point, each variation had adhered strictly to the sixteen-measure binary model with a half cadence on F at the midpoint and an authentic cadence onto B flat at the end. Variation 4 follows the model in B flat minor, but Farrenc seems to have determined that a stronger transition was needed to move the music back from minor to the tonic major to set up the final variation. The added material continues to repeat the triplet figuration from the variation, first in descending arpeggios played by the violin that lead to an unexpected D flat major sonority (III in B flat minor) in m. 83, then in a series of rising arpeggios played by the flute. The flute leads the ensemble through a cadential progression in B flat minor that stops on a long held dominant-seventh chord to prepare the return of the tonic at m. 89. On its own, this brief transition is not especially noteworthy. But for the players and audiences of Farrenc's day, it may have sounded somewhat familiar.

In the third movement "Andante con variazioni" of Hummel's Septet, the third and penultimate variation is in the movement's parallel minor (F minor), and it features triplet sixteenth-note figuration, as both Beethoven and Farrenc's minor-mode vari-ations do, here in the piano part that decorates a lightly altered version of the theme in the strings and winds. Hummel's Septet consistently highlights the pianist with brilliant passagework and melodically inventive variations; unlike Farrenc's later Nonet, it does not give much spotlighted time to the other instruments, who mostly accompany in the background of the work, giving the piece something of the "chamber concerto" style that was popular in piano chamber music of the early nineteenth century, especially in Paris. (Nineteenth-century virtuosos often performed scaled-down

Example 2.7 Hummel Septet, movement 3, mm. 112–128 (Variation 3).

versions of concertos, with the orchestra parts arranged for string quartet or quintet, in salon performances and other small venues. These performances and new compositions like the *quatuor brilliant* led to an entire repertoire of concerto-like works originally composed for chamber ensembles, such as the piano quintets of Hummel, Ferdinand Ries, and Johann Pixis. Chopin seems to have performed several of his piano-orchestral works in chamber arrangements in Warsaw and Paris in the 1830s.[26]) In Hummel's Septet, Variation 3 presents an extended cadential passage, shown in Ex. 2.7 (mm. 122–131), that momentarily brings the wind instruments to the forefront of the texture during an unprepared move to D flat (flat VI in this context). The music has cadenced onto F minor, and the horn enters with reiterated eighth notes that seem at first to confirm the new tonic; the timbre of the instrument recalls a hunting horn, intruding on the silence of this cadence. When the strings join the texture, they add a D flat and A flat, suddenly shifting the harmony down a third into the warm realm of a pastoral topic; the flute's gentle bird-like answer completes this minuscule outdoor scene. (The fortissimo fanfare that interrupts this moment in mm. 126–127 and moves the harmony abruptly from D flat to C major is a shortened version of the curious cadential "tag" Hummel includes at the ends of the theme and the first two variations; this is its last appearance in the movement.) This brief pastoral interlude prefaces an exploratory thematic extension that builds to a suspenseful dominant prolongation in mm. 132–146 and creates a strong sense of drama when the theme appears in its most highly decorated form at m. 148. Hummel's final variation repeats a curtailed version of this process on B flat in mm. 179–198 with a repetition of the evocative horn entrance on F after a strong cadence and a sudden modulation, now to the subdominant, when the strings and piano enter playing B flat and D. Hummel's Romantic modulations and introduction of a topical style strongly associated with the outdoors and with Romantic longing (e.g., the "Waldeinsamkeit," or solitude in the forest, celebrated in the poetry and prose of Eichendorff and Tieck) create drama and novelty at the end of his variations movement.

Farrenc used a similar technique to end her variations movement with a satisfying sense of closure and novelty, by introducing an abrupt move to the mediant (III, or D flat) at the end of her minor-mode variation followed by an extended cadential flourish and pregnant pause on V7 before moving on to the final variation. For audiences familiar with the Hummel Septet – a work that the Society for Classical Music had performed in December 1847 and again in March 1849 – this dramatic gesture probably sounded both familiar and exciting, perhaps creating for those connoisseurs a momentary recognition and connection between Farrenc and Hummel.

The movement ends with a gigue-like "Allegretto" variation in 6/8 time to bring the movement to a lively close in a style associated with folk dancing. The gigue, like the contredanse, was a French social dance imported from England; the gigue is the more formal French version of the raucous jig. It was the typical closing dance in suites and dance-based sonatas during the early eighteenth century and continued to be an important style for folk-inspired finale movements in the works of Haydn, Mozart, and Beethoven. After presenting the sixteen-measure contredanse theme transformed into its more lively cousin, the coda takes a last detour through flat VI (G flat) before the winds bring the work to a quiet close in the tonic. Farrenc's harmonic diversions are not as sensational as Hummel's, and her variations movement in general remains closely connected to the Classical aesthetic of balance and symmetry that critics and musicians of her day associated with Beethoven and Mozart. This preference for an older thematic style and the restrained approach to technical display in this work ally it with a conservative musical outlook and won Farrenc the accolades of audiences and critics at the time. At the December 1849 salon premiere, "the audience especially applauded an Andante with variations and a scherzo" within the work, according to the report in the *Revue et Gazette musicale*.[27] Farrenc's seemingly conservative approach to the variations procedures in this movement allowed her to focus on texture and timbre and to provide ample opportunities for the individual members of the ensemble to shine as soloists.

Movement 3: Scherzo Vivace

Whereas the Nonet's Variations movement shows a decidedly Classical, even old-fashioned, approach that linked Farrenc to important musical forebears, the third-movement Scherzo has an unmistakable Romantic verve and a flair for musical drama that connect it to works by Farrenc's contemporaries Mendelssohn and Chopin, as well as Hummel, Spohr, and Onslow. By the early nineteenth century, the scherzo had replaced the minuet as the preferred dance-like inner movement in multi-movement instrumental works. Formal designs and even meters varied from the

Table 2.3 *Overview of ternary form in Farrenc Nonet, movement 3 (Scherzo vivace).*

Scherzo Vivace 3/4 time	mm. 1–32	‖: mm. 33–80	81–114 :‖
	(A)	(B)	(A')
	Strings answered by winds;	Group crescendo to Hunt theme (mm. 49–64) and descresendo after	Variation on mm. 1–32, fortissimo in style of the Hunt theme
	C minor to G minor (v)	G major, E flat, G major	C minor
Meno mosso [Trio]	mm. 115–146	‖: mm. 147–174	175–201 :‖
	Reduced texture, emphasis on winds	Focused on strings	Return to winds (variation on mm. 115ff)
	C major, close on G (V)	Modulatory, move to A Major (VI)	C major
Scherzo Vivace	mm. 202–233	mm. 234–249	250–281
	[exact repetition of mm. 1–32]	[same as 33–80]	[same as 81–114]
[Coda]	mm. 308–334		
	Begins (A) theme, but sputters out		

1810s, with some famous scherzi in duple meter, and both Beethoven and Schubert sometimes abandoned the traditional binary dance structure in favor of sonata form in their more ambitious scherzo movements. But a common approach of fast tempos, strong contrasts, and an often light, humorous style suggested by the word "scherzo," or joke, remained key to the character and intentions of the style through the 1820s; it contrasted with the increasingly serious tone of outer movements in symphonies, sonatas, and chamber works. The Romantic generation that came to the forefront of musical life in the 1830s and 1840s transformed the relentless energy of earlier scherzos to a restless or nervous tone, both in movements within larger works and in free-standing publications or collections. Mendelssohn's famous "fairy scherzos" introduced a new level of suspense with the minor mode, quiet dynamics, and increasingly virtuosic speed and delicacy, as exemplified by the third movement of his youthful Octet, Op. 20 (1825), his concert overture inspired by Shakespeare's play *A Midsummer Night's Dream, Ein Sommernachtstraum*, Op. 21 (1826), and the Scherzo of his later incidental music for this play, Op. 61 (1842). With works like these and Chopin's three Scherzi, Opp. 20, 31, and 39 (published between 1835 and 1840), the minor-mode scherzo became more common, often used to evoke a frenzied supernatural or even demonic atmosphere. More pertinently for Farrenc, the Scherzo movements of the three most obvious models for her own Nonet – Hummel's Septet, Op. 74, Spohr's Nonet, Op. 31, and Onslow's Nonet, Op. 77 – are all in the minor mode. Both Onslow's and Hummel's Scherzo movements are in the home key of the work: A minor and D minor, respectively. Spohr's Scherzo is set in the relative minor, D minor in the work's home key of F major. In Mendelssohn's Octet for strings, the Scherzo movement is in G minor, or vi relative to the work's E flat major tonic. (Farrenc's two piano quintets composed in 1839 and 1840, Op. 30 and Op. 31, also include minor-mode Scherzo movements in a similar frenzied, demonic style typical of this Romantic tradition.)

The Nonet's Scherzo Vivace in C minor is structured in the traditional ternary form with a Scherzo section that is repeated after the Trio, which is marked "Meno mosso" (mm. 115–210) and followed by a brief coda (mm. 308 to 334). Both the Scherzo and the Trio are in rounded binary forms that create many opportunities to hear the opening theme in different treatments with different instrumentations. Demonstrating a decidedly Romantic approach to the scherzo that would be familiar to some listeners from the examples cited above, the opening theme is plucked out by the violin and cello in octaves, which creates tension and suspense in the piano dynamic (Ex. 2.8). This soft pizzicato line evokes a tiptoeing, secretive atmosphere that is enhanced when the viola joins the texture in mm. 9–16, filling in the rests with see-sawing two-note gestures. The winds answer with their own version of the sixteen-measure theme. Their variation fills in the rests to create

Example 2.8 Farrenc Nonet, movement 3, mm. 1–24 (Scherzo main theme).

a more confident sounding legato style, but the piano dynamic and minor mode maintain an air of watchful suspense, particularly when the theme closes for the second time with a weak half cadence on the minor dominant (G minor). The "B" section of the Scherzo begins with a prolongation of the dominant and a series of motivic gestures that create dissonant intervals against insistent, reiterated Gs in the horn and violin. The absence of a real melody in this section enhances the uncanny sense of expectant waiting.

When a boisterous hunting theme erupts from the texture at m. 49, it feels both unexpected (because the sudden E flat major tonality has been unprepared) and gratifyingly long-awaited because the harmony and texture have been building to a climactic revelation throughout mm. 33–48. This is the first time in the movement that the entire ensemble has played together, which gives the theme an added celebratory quality that is enhanced by the ringing diatonic sonorities and forte dynamic. The sixteen-measure theme in the horn and violin (Ex. 2.9) leaps around the tonic arpeggio in its first half,

96

Example 2.9 Farrenc Nonet, movement 3, mm. 47–64 ("Hunt" theme).

then through the supertonic (F minor, or ii in E flat) in the second half. The theme closes without a definitive cadence, but moves from ii to vi to III, arriving back at its entry point (not really its beginning) G major at m. 63. The hunting theme disappears as suddenly as it appeared, and the music immediately returns to a soft piano dynamic with a reduced texture to present choppy staccato motives over dominant harmony and a descending chromatic scale in parallel thirds that increases the Scherzo's creepy, secretive mood. In performances that presented this Scherzo immediately after the Andante second movement (not always the case in the nineteenth century, when programs often gave individual movements or dispersed the movements of a larger work throughout the program), the sudden appearance and disappearance of this hunting theme might also connect listeners back to the evocative Hummel example described earlier, when a hunting theme in the horn seems to intrude unexpectedly at the end of the third variation.

97

The final section of Farrenc's Scherzo (mm. 81–114) borrows some of the mood of the interpolated hunting theme, bringing the work back to a full ensemble texture and fortissimo dynamic for a new version of the opening material. This presentation highlights the similarity between the two themes' leaping arpeggios, though the difference of mode and instrumentation create wildly different stylistic associations. The opening theme's choppy motives in the violin and viola, paired with a descending scalar accompaniment in the cello and bass and sustained chords in the winds, continues to have an ominous, shadowy effect that connects to Romanticism's fascination with the macabre. Because the topical association of the hunting theme and horn suggest the outdoors, and specifically the forest, the effect of the Scherzo as a whole suggests a dark wood and a brief, startling encounter with a (perhaps supernatural?) huntsman who melts into the boughs as effortlessly and unexpectedly as he appeared.

The movement's Trio in C major switches to a serene pastoral style that contrasts with the tense Scherzo and recalls the atmosphere evoked by the brief hunting theme. The texture throughout this part of the movement is reduced, with no instances of full ensemble, which gives the Trio section a more intimate quality, as well. Each member of the group participates in one or more of the smaller ensemble textures, but the overall texture rarely exceeds four voices. The Trio's calm character comes, in part, from the continuous rippling accompaniment that underlies the lyrical main theme; the entire first section of the Trio is accompanied by the viola playing cascading eighth-note scales, and the violin takes up this accompaniment when the melody returns in mm. 175–193. The prominence of the wind instruments in the Trio, especially the clarinet and horn, also contributes to the bucolic, outdoorsy atmosphere. The main theme is a duet presented first by the oboe and clarinet in parallel thirds, then by the clarinet and horn in parallel sixths. These sonorities give the entire section an agreeable euphonious style often associated (in nineteenth-century opera and song, for example) with pleasure and leisure.

A brief, accelerating transitional passage reintroduces the Scherzo's racing pulse, choppy staccato motives, and minor mode to prepare an exact restatement of that portion of the work (omitting

98

the repeats). Farrenc opted to end the movement in the minor mode and in the Scherzo's tense mood by appending a short coda that recalls the movement's opening phrase, now played by the flute and clarinet. When the answering "b" material does not arrive, though, the unfinished theme seems to stall, and the full-measure rests of mm. 319 and 321 introduce a potentially comical element, as though the train of thought has been lost. Listeners and performers familiar with Haydn's humorous use of rests and silences, especially in fast-paced movements like finales, may hear this sudden absence as a fun, lighthearted joke between the ensemble members and the audience. (It recalls the finale of Haydn's most famous bit of musical fun, the Op. 33 No. 2 string quartet, nicknamed "the Joke," which closes with an episode filled with unexpected pauses and an incomplete statement of its opening theme that often causes audiences to believe the work is over before it is. Haydn played this game again in the finales of his string quartets Op. 50 No. 1 and Op. 76 No. 1.) Alternatively, performances may suggest a more macabre feeling of something or someone receding into the shadows, as though the theme becomes distant and muffled amid the trees of the forest before startling the audience with the string's final forte statement of G–C that punctuates the close of the movement.

Movement 4: Adagio – Allegro

The first three movements of the Nonet charm listeners with a balanced mixture of the familiar and the new. The opening movement is filled with lyrical melodies that extend and expand into surprising harmonic revelations through engaging dialogue among the players, but largely follows the plan of sonata form that established connoisseurs of chamber music would recognize from works they would have heard and played. The inner movements demonstrate Farrenc's dual persona as a studious composer capable of writing an elegant set of variations in the eighteenth-century style as well as a modern Romantic tone poet who could write a dramatic Scherzo in the style of more recent musical works. The finale of the Nonet closes the work in a grand style with a demonstration of both learned and lyrical writing that requires listeners (and players) to constantly reevaluate what they're hearing and the relationships between musical ideas. Much more so than the first movement, this sonata form poses a series of questions for the listener and is filled with variations and alterations of materials that change the nature of their function within the "normative" timelines of the exposition, development, and return of familiar materials. The movement contains no large-scale repeats (i.e., the exposition is not separated from the development section by a double bar repeat sign), which further blurs the boundaries between formal sections and requires listeners to reinterpret musical themes retrospectively as music continues to run forward without giving them an opportunity to rehear and reassess.

Although the broad outlines of the movement conform to Reicha's sonata form plan, as shown in Table 2.4, the formal relationships of individual musical ideas to the effect of the whole only become clear later in the work or on repeated listenings. For the more casual listeners who surely made up the bulk of Parisian audiences in the mid nineteenth century (and today), the effect of the movement might be a pleasant flurry of brilliant-style passagework that allows each player of the ensemble to shine in highlighted themes and dialogues with their compatriots. Like the first movement, the finale is filled with running eighth notes and motivic play that seem to spin on and on, developing and extending musical ideas from one line to the next and creating a breathtaking stream of continuous music with very few breaks. Analytical listeners in the modern day or among the devoted connoisseurs who attended Wartel's chamber performances with Joachim and Cossmann in 1850 and who frequented the Society for Classical Music's earlier concert series might have observed some unusual details in the succession of musical ideas. For example, the exposition lacks a clearly stated "mother idea" or theme in the second key (or, per Reicha, the "new tonic"), and presents in its place an extended development of materials from the bridge.

The movement is dominated by contrapuntal writing, with free counterpoint taking up the bulk of the first section and an imitative fugal treatment of themes from that part of the exposition in the developmental portion of the second section. This may have been

Table 2.4 *Overview of sonata form in Farrenc Nonet, movement 4 (Allegro).*

First part or exposition of ideas	*First motive, or "mother idea"*	*Bridge, or passage from one idea to another*	*Second mother idea in the new tonic*	*Accessory ideas and conclusion of the first part*
	mm. 6–36	mm. 37–53	mm. 54–68	mm. 69–93
	Rounded binary theme in E flat major	Contrapuntal theme, modulates from E flat to B flat	?? continued counterpoint in B flat ??	Closing theme over pedal tones (B flat and F) and fanfare-like cadences ending on B flat
First section of the second part	*Principal Development, constantly modulating*		*Stop on the original dominant*	
	mm. 94–138		mm. 139–151	
	Fugato based on contrapuntal theme (modulating)		"Retransition" over a dominant pedal (B flat), ending with unison passagework	
Second section of the second part	*Initial motive in the original key*	*Some tertiary modulations with ideas from the bridge*	*Transposition of the second key in the original key, with modifications*	*Coda*
	mm. 152–178	mm. 179–210	mm. 211–252	mm. 253–286
	Rounded binary theme in E flat major	New material in A flat major, modulating through B flat and G flat before arriving again at B flat	material from mm. 54–68; modulatory, but in E flat after m. 228	New material with virtuosic high-tessitura passagework for the violin, then lighter passagework for the rest of the ensemble

considered a risky move in the late 1840s, given Parisian listeners's documented disdain for learned instrumental styles. (Thérèse Wartel's and Bernard Cossmann's performance of a Mendelssohn duo for cello and piano had been coolly received a couple of years earlier for this reason, as noted in Chapter 1.) Rather than merely avoid contrapuntal writing in a bow to Parisian taste, Farrenc found ways to incorporate it within a light, effervescent style in the Nonet finale. The learned style of contrapuntal writing in this movement connects the Nonet to the serious classical style that critics and musicians associated with chamber music (and with German or Viennese instrumental traditions), while the textural variety and instrumentation of the work lends it a charming, virtuosic character. The finale is filled with musical dialogue that gives the whole movement the quality of listening to an exciting skit or debate. Even in the contrapuntal and fugal sections it deploys a brilliant style of sparkling passagework familiar from many post-Classical showpieces by Hummel, Pixis, and Weber, but it never ventures into over-the-top virtuosity, and the opportunities for technical display are spread throughout the ensemble, rather than concentrated in one or two voices.

Despite the unusual character of the musical ideas it presents, the exposition, which starts in m. 6 after the brief Adagio introduction, divides neatly into three easily identifiable sections made clear with textural cues. The opening theme is a sunny, vivacious rounded binary melody that unfolds in a leisurely fashion over twenty-six measures (mm. 10–34). It features first the violin, then the clarinet, as soloists against a playful backdrop in the rest of the ensemble. This breezy theme is idiomatic for the instruments with ornaments and passagework that combine with the symmetrical melodic contour to create a memorable, slightly folk-like instrumental tune. This theme ends with a strong cadence in the tonic (E flat), followed by a half-measure rest in m. 36 that reinforces the sense of a strong close. As is often the case in the earlier style of Mozart and his contemporaries, that silence both cues the listener that new and important music is about to begin and gives the performers a moment to breathe and refocus their attention for the passage coming up. The contrasting theme that follows the cadence and rest at m. 36 presents a stark contrast to what we have

Example 2.10 Farrenc Nonet, movement 4, mm. 37–54 (contrapuntal bridge or second mother idea).

heard so far, though it begins in the E flat of the previous cadence (see Ex. 2.10). The theme's austere presentation in octaves with gaping leaps in the melody and rhythmic acceleration – it begins with half-notes, moves through a series of clipped quarter-note motives, then closes with an eighth-note flourish, creating the sense of increasing speed as the theme approaches its cadence onto B flat – all combine to suggest the opening of a fugue or canon. For those familiar with the musicians participating in the Nonet's premiere, a fugal passage might not be unexpected, given both Joachim's and Farrenc's propensity to perform "ancient music" by Handel and Bach, which critics had noted in previous reviews of both musician's Paris performances. (As he often did, Joachim gave the Bach D-minor Chaconne as a solo encore at the end of the March 1850 performance of the Nonet.) This passage does not develop into an imitative fugato-style section at this juncture in the Nonet; rather, it starts a long passage of free counterpoint. The subsequent thematic entrances continue in the theme's purposeful, forward-propelled style, and the contrapuntal texture created by weaving these independent themes together differentiates this section from the homophony of the opening melody.

The free counterpoint heard in this portion of the movement begins in the tonic (E flat) and modulates to the dominant (B flat), but as soon as we arrive at B flat, the music switches back to the tonic, transforms to E flat minor, and moves through a circle-of-fifth progression that uses all nine players in mm. 63–68. The passage's sudden shift to a full-textured chordal style in whole and half notes appears designed to catch the listeners' attention, and it marks a seam in the form. Reicha's "accessory ideas and conclusion of the first part," or closing material, begins the final or third section of the exposition. This portion of the movement (mm. 69–93) repeatedly confirms the new tonic with cadential progressions in B flat. It alternates between reduced-texture passages of dialogue between two or three instruments and full-ensemble confirmations of the key in a fanfare style. Another full rest (this one notated as three beats) in m. 93 marks the end of the exposition. At no point in the performance of the larger middle portion of the exposition do the players present a clearly delineated theme that characterizes the new key. The entire section proceeds breathlessly from the opening motif of the contrapuntal theme at m. 37 until the next grand pause at m. 93. Along the way, new countermelodies are introduced to complement the contrapuntal theme, and motives are repeated at the ends of phrases to extend the musical materials into new harmonic territory. The combination of instruments constantly shifts, creating a diverse palette of timbres in this long span of continuous counterpoint.

The status of this contrapuntal section as a "mother idea" (not as a bridge or transition, despite its highly modulatory style) is clarified somewhat by the development that follows in mm. 94–151. The second section of the movement begins with a contrapuntal presentation of the fugato-like theme from m. 37, thereby fulfilling the expectation that the mother ideas of the exposition will generate motives and materials for further development later in the piece but

Example 2.11 Farrenc Nonet, movement 4, mm. 94–123 (fugue in the development section).

sidestepping the lyrical theme from the first mother idea. In this instance, the contrapuntal theme does initiate a full fugal style imitative process. Example 2.11 highlights the entries of the theme/subject and its variations at different levels of transposition. It begins with an unprepared direct modulation from the dominant harmony (B flat) that closed the exposition to a sudden G major chord in m. 94 that leads to the fugal subject's entry in C minor; subsequent answers move to D flat major, then through F minor and B flat minor to arrive at F (V of V in the movement's home key) in m. 123. The fugal section ends here, when the strings play a homorhythmic reiteration of the dominant chord, then cycle through a series of distantly related flat-side harmonies that surround a long passage of eighth-note arpeggios for the violin. Farrenc signals the expected "stop on the original dominant" at m. 139 with a B flat pedal, then an impressive fast-paced unison passage for the strings (mm. 144–151) that outlines the progression V, V of V, V7 to prepare the return of the opening theme in the tonic at m. 152.

How did Farrenc make a long and learned section of contrapuntal writing palatable to French audiences who tended to prefer simpler textures? First, she placed contrapuntal materials at the transition or bridge and in the development section, positions in the movement where such motivic work and modulatory motion are expected. Although the absence of a second mother idea in the exposition makes this material, by default, a bridge to nowhere thematically, it brings the music and the listener from one key to another, which was the more important aspect of the form for French listeners and theorists in the first half of the nineteenth century. Second, the textural play and focus on musical dialogue give both contrapuntal sections a strong theatrical quality, especially since the countersubject that recurs throughout both sections in altered forms provides opportunities to hear (and see) flashy passagework travel throughout the ensemble and to appreciate the diversity of tone colors of the wind and string instruments and the technical skills of the players. In the development section's fugue, for example, the running eighth notes begin in the violin, are picked up by the cello, then the clarinet, the viola, and then return to the violin, creating a dazzling play of tone colors around the layered entrances of the main subject in other voices. The subject's statement by the bassoon and double bass in octaves at m. 111, similarly, provides a rare opportunity to hear melodic playing from those instruments, increasing the technical appeal of the passage. (The bassoon repeats the theme at m. 118, transposed up a sixth, with the viola doubling in the same octave; punctuated by rising scales in the cello and bass, this whole passage has the effect of showing off the melodic potential of the low-tessitura members of the ensemble.) Finally, because the initial contrapuntal section is not imitative and because the fugal development contains a lengthy episode (a portion of the fugue without a statement of the subject) just after the theme is introduced, neither can be described as strict or academic in tone. Although they display a learned compositional mastery, neither section revels in the exacting intricacies of counterpoint or imitation for their own sake. Instead, each section offers a rich exploration of the many timbres and textures available in this large-ensemble format and honors the soloistic and dialogic nature that is a defining feature of chamber music. These aspects of the work must have resonated with the connoisseurs attending Farrenc's soirée in 1850, and they would certainly have been appreciated by the audiences of the Society for Classical Music series and similar audiences at exclusive chamber-music concerts in this era.

The final big section of the work (the recapitulation) provides further indication of Farrenc's awareness of her audience's tastes because it does not recall the head motifs from the contrapuntal materials or the fugal theme presented earlier in the movement. Instead, it offers new musical ideas combined with familiar motives from elsewhere in the work, recomposed to highlight elements that had been submerged in the busy textures of the exposition. This continual development is a hallmark of Farrenc's chamber style; her two piano quintets and piano trios also regularly feature explorations of motives and themes that extend developmental activity into the late portions of the work. (It also demonstrates Reicha's suggestion that the entire second half of a sonata form falls into the "development" of ideas, including the return of materials in the final section. Reicha's instruction on how to develop musical ideas suggest that the reimagining of motives from the exposition in new and different roles is a major indicator of compositional skill.[28]) The recapitulation also provides space for Farrenc to recompose elements from the exposition in terms of their formal functions, perhaps even to "correct" the order and presentation of materials to better align with listener expectations. In effect, Farrenc presents a "problem" or challenge to prevailing conventions in the first half of the work and then reveals a "solution" in the second half. The finale, therefore, offers a more dramatic version of sonata form than Reicha's description might indicate.

The finale's recapitulation presents a much more conventional version of the exposition's materials by altering the transition and the section devoted to the second key. Whereas the exposition presented a straightforward homophonic primary theme, a full stop, then free counterpoint with an austere, fugue-like subject, the recapitulation begins with the primary theme and then spins out new material from that theme's ending. The new transitional material that replaces the original contrapuntal theme from m. 37 (see Ex. 2.12) behaves the way transitional material "should" (based on prior experience with the Classical repertoire) whereas the exposition's material had disrupted the usual functional roles of the mother ideas and bridge. Starting with the reharmonization of the theme's final cadence to end on a secondary dominant (E flat 7, or V7 of IV), the new transition reinterprets that closing gesture as a continuation and develops it further through transpositions and repetitions, placing the motive in the bassoon and viola while other members of the ensemble provide supporting harmonies either in the same rhythms or in longer held tones.

When a new musical idea in B flat (V of the home tonic) arrives at m. 186, again in the bassoon, Farrenc provides another example of a more typical transition section, compared to the contrapuntal episode of the exposition. As though preparing for a strong cadence and arrival of a second theme in the new key, this bridge theme slows musical time on two fronts. (Refer back to Ex. 2.12.) Rhythmically, the transitional phrase uses slower rhythms: quarter notes and dotted half notes in the theme, supported with mostly long tones, often tied across bar lines, in the accompaniment. These create a calmer, almost languid atmosphere for the new bridge after the forward-pressing materials that preceded it. Harmonically, the theme and the developmental extensions that follow in mm. 196–205 pause for a few measures on the harmonic path toward the dominant by introducing an enharmonically spelled flat VI (B major, or C flat major – Farrenc's manuscript score simultaneously notates this passage with flats in the wind

Example 2.12 Farrenc Nonet, movement 4, mm. 176–216 (new transition material in the recapitulation and second mother idea rescored).

parts and sharps in the strings); this "purple patch" functions as a sort of harmonic cul-de-sac. The move to flat VI, brief though it is, carries the listener away from a goal-directed trajectory and into an alternative tonal space outside of the diatonic realm of E flat major. As noted earlier, in relation to a similar gambit in the first movement, this is a regular technique used by early Romantic composers (that generation of composers, including Schubert, first impacted by new narrative approaches around the turn of the nineteenth century) to effect a sudden change of perspective or setting, or to evoke the fantastic or supernatural. It is most notable in Schubert's works after 1820 and in operatic scenes from the 1830s, though it shows up as well in the music of Chopin and later in Brahms. (In the course of an extended aria or

Example 2.12 (cont.)

duet, Rossini, Donizetti, and Bellini often moved from introductory recitative in the scene's tonic to a third-related key such as flat VI or flat III for a slow-tempo, contemplative aria or "Cavatina," followed by modulatory recitative or action that leads to a fast-tempo finale or "Cabaletta" in the home key.[29]) Unlike Schubert or Rossini, though, Farrenc does not introduce new lyrical thematic material here; instead, the music cycles through a slow-moving arch-shaped arpeggiated passage in the violin and long tones in the rest of the voices before finding its way back to B flat major and the actual prolongation of dominant harmony with scalar runs exchanged by several members of the ensemble. The main effect of this purple patch is a sudden slowing of musical time to cleanse the musical palate. It prepares the listener and performer to hear the music that follows with new clarity.

The recollection and rescoring of some materials first heard in the original contrapuntal section highlights a more recognizable "second mother idea" that had been present, but largely over-shadowed in the exposition. Here, too, we can discern Farrenc "correcting" or clarifying relationships between materials to create a recapitulation that more easily aligns with audience expectations and demonstrates her compositional skill – the "hidden" second mother idea is revealed to listeners in the recapitulation, which prompts a reevaluation of this music's role in the overall form. Music theorist Janet Schmalfeldt has explored the idea of listeners creating and altering their understanding of musical elements or materials during the course of the performance (or on repeated listening) as new information emerges in the listening process. In Farrenc's music, as in some works of her immediate predecessors in the early decades of the nineteenth century, we can hear "form coming into being" through the interactive nature of listening with specific formal models in mind.[30]

In the Nonet finale's exposition, the music that begins around m. 54 reinforces motion from F or F7 to B flat, creating relative harmonic stability, but its thematic and motivic profile is not significantly differentiated from the preceding material. When this material returns in the recapitulation, though, several changes give it a stronger "theme-like" quality (refer back to Ex. 2.12). Most notably, the lead-in to the theme in this version marks its entrance or recollection more clearly as an important event. In its first appearance, the second theme had been preceded by some transitional motives in the violin and viola with a reiterated F in the clarinet, whose slow trill (the F–G alternation in quarter notes, mm. 52–53) gives the lead-in an almost agitated style and maintains the momentum of the earlier contrapuntal material. In the recapitulation, however, the newly composed transition described above begins to slow musical time with its flat VI diversion and slower rhythmic values, then musical time effectively stops at m. 211 and stands still on the dominant. A short ensemble silence and a long-held B flat in the clarinet line create a sense of suspended animation. The legato component of the "theme" that had earlier been played by the viola and cello beneath the clarinet's scalar runs now lies above that passagework, played by the flute and oboe, which gives it a stronger presence in the texture. The clarinet's line, which had seemed like the melody over a chordal accompaniment in m. 54–58 now sounds more like a decorative addition to a short, slow-moving melody in parallel thirds. As is often the case in the Nonet, Farrenc's choice of scoring in these two instances enhances the divergence in listener perception. In the recapitulation, the second mother idea belongs to a wind trio without accompaniment from the strings, which sets it apart from the surrounding full-ensemble material and clarifies its narrative importance to the unfolding of the movement's form. This late revelation of the second musical idea is followed by a recapitulation of closing ideas, including a transposed version of the circle-of-fifth progression from earlier, starting now on A-flat minor and ending neatly on the tonic in m. 228 (in second inversion, a cadential 6/4 chord) and m. 232 (in root position).

The end of the recapitulation and the coda provide some last opportunities for the violinist to shine in fast, high passagework, perhaps a nod to Parisian's love of virtuosity and the desire to see a star violinist display their skill in the big finish of a program's centerpiece. The transitional flourish of mm. 243–244 replaces a memorable syncopated eighth-note cadential passage from the end of the exposition with a noticeably flashier version in triplets that climbs higher, ending on B flat well above the staff. In similar fashion, the coda begins with a fast triplet motive tossed around the ensemble in mm. 253–256, then the violin takes over the musical idea with a four-measure phrase of scalar triplets that climb into the instrumental stratosphere before cascading down to a rest on the tonic in m. 262. Although it makes a powerful impression of virtuosity, this passage does not end the work.

Rather, the full ensemble engages in another exchange of motives that reinforce motion from the dominant to the tonic before closing with punctuating tonic chords in the final four measures of the piece. Here as throughout the Nonet, Farrenc privileges the ensemble experience and impresses on the listener the image of a community of equals, rather than a solo-led concertante-style work for one or two star players.

Another way to understand the balance that Farrenc negotiates in this movement is in terms of its "end-weightedness," or the nature of this movement's relationship to the work as a whole. In his study of instrumental finales, Michael Talbot identifies several approaches to ending a multi-movement work common in the eighteenth, nineteenth, and twentieth centuries. The most common approach is the "relaxant" finale, which provides a light ("short, simple, and sometimes humorous") close.[31] Despite its connotations of learnedness and weightiness, which goes against the tendency to provide a light ending to a large work, fugal writing has long been associated with finales in concert music, especially chamber music and symphonies, where it offers an opportunity for the full ensemble to come together in a display of equity and camaraderie. Talbot notes that fugal writing also easily lent itself to humor and parody, especially when combined with comic gestures, as was often the case in the works of Haydn and Mozart. Other aspects of Farrenc's Nonet finale align it with this "light" style of ending: It is about half the length in performance time of the opening sonata form movement and uses a folksy, motivic style in the tonic theme, as opposed to the more lyrical style of the first movement's first and second themes. But the counterpoint of Farrenc's movement seems sincere; she does not introduce counterthemes that contradict the learned style of the subject or introduce elements from opera buffa, and although she does introduce brilliant-style ensemble passagework she does not juxtapose the fugato style with brazenly virtuosic or dance-like themes as though to demonstrate two extremes. Elements of the finale's structure and tone suggest it should be understood as a "summative" ending, a more "weighty" movement, often in an unconventional form, that "aims to sum up the cycle as a whole."[32] The combination of contrapuntal writing in the exposition and development with the recomposition (or, continued development) of motives and themes in the recapitulation give this movement the quality of a demonstration of skills. Throughout the Nonet, Farrenc shows her familiarity with the musical structures and conventions of the recent past and of her own day, with the repertoire of the Nonet specifically and of popular chamber music in Paris more generally, and with the capabilities of the instruments and performers for whom she wrote the Nonet. The finale sums up this demonstration with a *tour de force* of compositional skill, presented in the style of a light, celebratory close. In this way, it demonstrates a hybrid finale type, or a movement with a "relaxant quality" despite its "summative weight."

* * *

Although many elements connect the Nonet for Winds and Strings to Farrenc's reputation as a serious "classical" composer, it is also clearly an expression of Romantic sensibilities regarding form and harmony, with many resonances between it and the forward-looking chamber music of Schubert, Mendelssohn, and Schumann. Perhaps that is why this work continued to make a strong impression on listeners in the 1850s and afterwards among Paris's most respected musicians and critics, leading in the 1860s to Farrenc's well-earned recognition by France's national Academy of Fine Arts.

Notes

1. Antoine Reicha, *Traité de Mélodie, Abstraction faite de ses rapports avec l'harmonie* (Paris: l'Auteur, 1814); and Reicha, *Traité de haute composition musicale* (Paris: Zetter, 1826).
2. Simon P. Keefe, "Antoine Reicha's 'Dialogue': The Emergence of a Theoretical Concept" *Acta Musicologica* 72/1 (2000): 43–62.
3. Warren Darcy and James Hepokoski, *Elements of Sonata Theory: Norms, Types, and Deformations in the Late-Eighteenth-Century Sonata* (Oxford: Oxford University Press, 2006). For an accessible and updated introduction to Sonata Theory that also takes into account the abundant work that has been done by later scholars to add nuance to this method, see James Hepokoski, *A Sonata Theory Handbook* (Oxford: Oxford University Press, 2021).
4. See also Christin Heitmann, *Die Orchester- und Kammermusik von Louise Farrenc vor dem Hintergrund der zeitgenössischen Sonatentheorie* (Wilhelmshaven: Florian Noetzel, 2002).

5. "La première partie de cette coupe est l'exposition du morceau. La première section eu est l'intrigue, ou le noeud. La seconde section en est le dénouement." Reicha, *Traité de Haute Composition Musicale*, 298.

6. "Après avoir employé ce que le développement offre de plus intéressant, et après avoir parcouru une série de tons, en s'arrête communément sur la dominante primitive, sur laquelle on fait souvent une pédale suivie d'un conduit pour attaquer la section suivante." Ibid.

7. "On couronne le morceau par une Coda intéressante." Ibid., 299.

8. "Ce second motif est en LA. On peut faire sur lui les mêmes remarques que sur le motif initial, sauf que la répétition peut se faire aussi on La mineur lorsqu'on désire le répéter." Ibid., 298.

9. Marx, *Die Lehre von der musikalischen Komposition*, 2nd edn. (1848), edited and translated by Scott Burnham in *Musical Form in the Age of Beethoven: Selected Writings on Theory and Method* (Cambridge: Cambridge University Press, 1997): 273.

10. Susan McClary, *Feminine Endings: Music, Gender, and Sexuality* (Minneapolis: University of Minnesota Press, 1991), revised, 2002; Marcia Citron, *Gender and the Musical Canon* (Cambridge and New York: Cambridge University Press, 1993); Scott Burnham, "A. B. Marx and the Gendering of Sonata Form" in Ian Bent (ed.), *Music Theory in the Age of Romanticism* (Cambridge: Cambridge University Press, 1996): 163–186.

11. William O'Hara, "The Composer as Master of All Developments" in *Antoine Reicha and the Making of the Nineteenth-Century Composer* (Bologna: Orpheus, 2021): 115–152. See also Peter A. Hoyt, "The Concept of *développment* in the Early Nineteenth Century" in *Music Theory in the Age of Romanticism* (Cambridge: Cambridge University Press, 1996): 141–162.

12. Hepokoski, *A Sonata Theory Handbook*, 78.

13. Donald Francis Tovey, *Essays in Musical Analysis*, 6 vols. (London: Oxford University Press, 1935–1939); Charles Rosen, *The Classical Style: Haydn, Mozart, Beethoven*, expanded 2nd edn. (New York: Norton, 1997). On Schenkerian analysis, see Carl Schachter, *Unfoldings: Essays in Schenkerian Theory and Analysis* (New York: Oxford University Press 1999) or Allen Cadwallader and David Gagné, *Tonal Analysis: A Schenkerian Approach* (New York: Oxford University Press, 2007).

14. Burnham, "Introduction: Music and Spirit" in *Musical Form in the Age of Beethoven*, 1–14.

15. William Caplin, *Classical Form: A Theory of Formal Functions for the Instrumental Music of Haydn, Mozart, and Beethoven* (New York: Oxford University Press, 1998). For succinct summaries of recent applications of this theory in studies of nineteenth-century music, see

Steven Vande Moortele, "In Search of Romantic Form" *Music Analysis* 32/3 (2013): 404–431; and Moortele, "Romantic Forms" in Benedict Taylor (ed.), *The Cambridge Companion to Music and Romanticism* (Cambridge: Cambridge University Press, 2021): 258–276.

16. Anne Hyland, *Schubert's String Quartets: The Teleology of Lyric Form* (Cambridge: Cambridge University Press, 2023).

17. Ibid.

18. Xavier Hascher, "Schubert's Reception in France: A Chronology (1828–1928)" in *The Cambridge Companion to Schubert*, ed. Christopher H. Gibbs (Cambridge: Cambridge University Press, 1997): 263–269.

19. Keefe, "Antoine Reicha's 'Dialogue,'" 50.

20. Tovey, "Haydn's Chamber Music," originally published in *Cobbett's Cyclopedic Survey of Chamber Music* (1929), which is discussed and contextualized in Alexander Raymond Ludwig, "Expecting the Unexpected: Haydn's Three-Part Expositions" *Lumen* 32 (2013): 31–40. See also James Webster, "Schubert's Sonata Form and Brahms's First Maturity" *19th-Century Music* 2/1 (1978): 18–35.

21. Leonard Ratner, *Classic Music: Expression, Form, and Style* (New York: Schirmer, 1980): 225–228; and Rosen, *Sonata Forms* (New York: Norton, 1980): 255–261.

22. Barry S. Brook, "The Symphonie Concertante: Its Musical and Sociological Bases" *International Review of the Aesthetics and Sociology of Music* 6 (1975): 9–28.

23. Pierre Rode, *Selected String Quartets*, ed. Sam Girling, *Recent Researches in the Music of the Nineteenth and Early Twentieth Centuries*, No. 87 (Middleton, WI: A-R Editions, 2023); Girling, "'One for the Rode': The Contribution of Pierre Rode and the Quatuor Brillant to the Early Nineteenth-Century String Quartet" in *String Quartets in Beethoven's Europe*, ed. Nancy November (Brighton: Academic Studies Press, 2022): 207–227.

24. Holly Watkins, *Metaphors of Depth in German Musical Thought: From E. T. A. Hoffmann to Arnold Schoenberg* (Cambridge: Cambridge University Press, 2011).

25. Reicha, *Traité de haute composition*, 303–304.

26. On the virtuosic piano quintet, see Sumner Lott, "Negotiation Tactics" (2010); Halina Goldberg, "Chamber Arrangements of Chopin's Concert Works" *Journal of Musicology* 19/1 (2002): 39–84; and Goldberg, *Music in Chopin's Warsaw* (Oxford: Oxford University Press, 2008).

27. "Nouvelles," *Revue et Gazette musicale de Paris* 16/52 (December 30, 1849): 416.

28. William O'Hara, "The Composer as Master of All Developments," 129–133.
29. Scholar Philipp Gossett used the phrase "multipart form" for this procedure; see Harold S. Powers, "'La Solita forma' and 'The Uses of Convention'" *Acta Musicologica* 59/1 (1987): 65–90. On the interpretive connotations of Schubert's move to third-related keys in his late chamber works, see Sumner Lott, *The Social Worlds of Nineteenth-Century Chamber Music* (Urbana and Chicago: University of Illinois Press, 2015), 95–106.
30. Janet Schmalfeldt, *In the Process of Becoming* (Oxford: Oxford University Press, 2010).
31. Michael Talbot, *The Finale in Western Instrumental Music* (Oxford: Oxford University Press, 2007), 50.
32. Ibid.

RECEPTION AND LEGACY OF FARRENC'S NONET

By the end of the evening on March 19, 1850, the audience had heard a piano trio by Louise Farrenc, her new Nonet, and probably a selection of solos and songs – two or three excerpts of popular operas sung by a guest vocalist and two or three "light" instrumental works, like the Fantasy on Scottish airs that flutist Louis Dorus played on several of her soirées in the 1850s. The program closed with a performance of Farrenc's newly composed Sonata in C Minor for Piano and Violin, which would later be published as Op. 37, played by Joachim and Farrenc. The audience was transfixed by Joachim's passionate performance in the slow middle movement, whose second section features tense, fiery repeated chords in the piano beneath the violin's lyrical theme in a minor key before settling back into the sweeter, symmetrical melodies of the outer sections in the major tonic. By the time the resounding applause died away after this work, it must have been past ten o'clock, and Joachim had been playing nearly nonstop for at least two hours. The violin parts of the trio, the nonet, and the sonata require exceptional focus and artistic leadership, given the prominence of the violin in the textures of all three works, so he must have been tired, if also exhilarated by the crowd's support and enthusiasm. Ever a generous guest, the young soloist obliged the crowd with an encore befitting the scholarly renown of his hostess, his own rising reputation as a serious artist, and the cultivated tastes of the audience before him. He played the Chaconne from J. S. Bach's Partita No. 2 in D Minor, BWV 1004, for Solo Violin (composed c. 1720), a virtuoso solo of exquisite beauty and concentrated musical intensity that, due to its status as "ancient music" authored by Bach, also expressed a deep connection to the classical tradition of learned music. Around thirteen minutes long in most modern performances, the Chaconne presents a series of variations that incrementally increase in technical brilliance and contrapuntal complexity, showcasing the abilities of both the performer and the composer (and perhaps presenting a challenge for tired listeners, as the theme itself becomes obscured through the technical machinations of double- and triple-stops, polyphonic diminutions, and harmonics). The audience was riveted. Most of them probably were hearing this work for the first time; while a select few had, perhaps, heard it played by other virtuoso violinists as a curiosity, the work remained a rarity. As a capstone to the concert, it linked the young soloist, his supremely talented hostess, and the compositions that had been premiered on the concert to a legacy of great (German) instrumental works and their revival in the mid-nineteenth century.

The evening was described as a complete success. In her review of the concert published the following week in the *Revue et Gazette musicale*, Thérèse Wartel speculates that "Madame Farrenc must have been very happy with the great success of this evening; it will have shown her the sympathies of the public for serious and pure works, which we regrettably hear too rarely."[1] Even when we account for the fact that Wartel was a friend of the composer and players, apt to write favorably about the work and its performance due to her vested interest in the concert's success (this was common at the time; most concerts were written up by critics who were friends or close acquaintances of the host or composer in nineteenth-century Paris or who were employed by publishers with a financial interest in the work's success), the appreciative buzz that this concert generated around Farrenc and her compositions continued well after the hall had emptied that evening, suggesting genuine excitement and enthusiasm that led to further performances and accolades. The journal *La France musicale* published a review of the concert almost two months later that called it "one of the most interesting [concerts] of the season" and said that it "left a lasting impression."[2]

The work and the concert as a whole was such a success that it had to be repeated, and each repetition of the Nonet alongside a bevy of quality compositions by Farrenc brought more critical acclaim and incredulity that her music, especially her symphonic music, was not heard more often in other venues. A year after the Nonet's public premiere, in March 1851, Farrenc reconvened the

Society for Classical Music's core members to participate in her annual solo concert. Her colleagues from the Paris Conservatory Jean-Delphin Alard and Auguste Franchomme (collaborators in their own string quartet ensemble and well respected chamber musicians with whom Farrenc played on other occasions) took up the violin and cello parts, respectively, and the rest of the ensemble included those who had performed the Nonet with Joachim a year earlier: Casimir Ney (viola), Gouffé (bass), Dorus (flute), the Verroust brothers (oboe and bassoon), Leroy (clarinet), and Rousselot (horn). In addition to this encore of the Nonet, the program that night included several opportunities to hear Farrenc perform her own compositions. With her collaborators, she played three movements from her first piano quintet, Op. 30; a sonata for piano and violin (probably the second sonata, Op. 39); and a set of variations on a theme by Bellini for three pianos, Op. 29, that closed the concert in a grand style and allowed Farrenc to show off her triple talents as a composer, pianist, and teacher when she played it with two of her students.[3] Adrien de La Fage's review noted that "the three works she performed were extremely popular with the entire audience."[4] After noting that, "in such a concert, the singing part could only be incidental," de la Fage closes his review with an extended summary of Farrenc's compositional style that highlights her connection to the classical tradition:

Let's return for a moment to Madame Farrenc. I will not speak of her execution, everyone knows that it is irreproachable; but is there not just as much reason to admire the talent, so solid and so wise, that she was able to acquire in composition? The only reproach to address to her is that she is perhaps a little too sober about these happy boldnesses, these bursts of enthusiasm which make the artist forgive even aberrations in which the certainty of Madame Farrenc's taste would absolutely prevent her from being carried away. The dominant merit in her is naturalness and grace; she is from the school of Haydn, but she had Hummel as her master. She succeeds wonderfully in the scherzo, and who would be surprised? However serious a woman may be, she always likes to joke, and I would never reproach her for joking too often. Another quality of Madame Farrenc's talent is that she knows how to give the right proportion to the development of her thoughts, so that we never have to address to her the reproach that even the immortal Beethoven has not always escaped: "It's good, but it's too long."

Let us add that Mme Farrenc is almost the only one in France who still cultivates high instrumental music, with which composers no longer concern themselves. We have talked a lot about the future, the future of women for the reform of humanity; I would still find myself happy if its mission, to continue speaking the language of the day, was limited to bringing the other half of the human race back to good music, good taste and perhaps also to common sense.[5]

De La Fage and his contemporaries continued to opine, often with some surprise, that a woman like Farrenc could be the savior of the classical instrumental tradition in France. Like Wartel, de La Fage and subsequent critics writing about Farrenc's performances and her compositions decried the scarcity of new instrumental works in the traditional forms and praised Farrenc not only for filling the void but for doing so with excellently crafted and emotionally engaging works in that style.

In October 1855, Farrenc offered the Nonet again with most of the usual core ensemble, including Charles Lebouc on cello, and a Monsieur Barthélemy playing oboe. This concert was a benefit for a visiting singer Valentine Bianchi, one of the many young artists with whom Aristide and Louise Farrenc cultivated a warm mutually beneficial relationship during this era. (Aristide would assist Bianchi on a concert tour in German cities in December, during which he advocated for performances of his wife's orchestral music in meetings with conductors and musicians to no avail and sought out manuscripts and original sources for his own academic work.) Farrenc's pupils played a chamber version of her Wallenburg Variations, Op. 25 (originally for piano and orchestra) and the set of variations on a theme of Bellini for three pianos that had made a strong impression in earlier concerts. In his published review, Henri Blanchard singled out the Nonet, which opened the concert:

What can I say about this work? That if Madame Farrenc had not already written excellent symphonies, this nonetto, a symphony with a small footprint, would put her on the path, and make the many supporters of her talent wish that she would devote herself to this beautiful genre of music which is the true lyrical, instrumental drama. In this concert, which was as much hers as that of the young singer, this first among the female composers like no other country has, performed in various aspects, and often in a remarkable manner. Chamber music in the severe and pure style; in variations, for one and several pianos, of the fashionable kind; in an Italian opera aria, a *Didone* [*Abbandonata*], where Madame Farrenc was rightly applauded, both for her writing talent, and in the person of the excellent pianists she trained through her lessons.[6]

Ten years later, in December 1865, Farrenc's former pupil and patron Sophie Pierson-Bodin programmed the Nonet on her musical matinée, at which it "electrified the audience," according to one reviewer, who also remarked, "The more we know Madame Farrenc's compositions, the more we are surprised that her symphonies are not part of the repertoire of our large orchestra concerts; true amateurs [meaning here "music lovers," rather than dilettantes] are all the more eager to seize the opportunities offered to them to hear her chamber music."[7] Pierson-Bodin's matinée demonstrates the same programming approach that Farrenc and Wartel used in their concerts: She surrounded the Nonet with classical works by established "German" masters that, nonetheless, provided abundant opportunities for virtuosic display. She performed "the variations of Fr. Schubert in quintet" (presumably the fourth movement alone of Schubert's Trout Quintet, D. 667); Mozart's Kegelstatt Trio for piano, clarinet, and viola, K. 498; and excerpts from a Beethoven piano sonata. A "varied aria" for solo violin closed the program.[8] In this company, the Nonet shined as a modern example of serious music anchored in the techniques and style of Mozart, Schubert, and Beethoven.

The Nonet Leads to Wider Recognition of Farrenc's Accomplishments

The common thread among these reviews of the Nonet – that it demonstrated Farrenc's learnedness, her talent for composing with naturalness, grace, and with a strong sense of proportion and reason that were typical of the classical tradition, and especially that it served as a reminder of her excellent work as a symphonist – shows that the critics and music lovers of Paris felt that Farrenc had been unfairly overlooked by and excluded from the official musical institutions of France. Her symphonies were being played in Brussels, Copenhagen, and other cities to a glowing reception with audiences, musicians, and critics, but only her Symphony No. 3 in G minor had so far received Paris's official stamp of approval through performance at the Société des Concerts du Conservatoire in 1849, and it was not repeated in her lifetime. She had arranged a performance of her second symphony in 1846 during a special solo concert that she organized at the Conservatory's large recital hall with an orchestra led by Theophile Tilmant.[9] Aristide's short-lived Société symphonique performed one of Louise's symphonies (probably the third) in 1851. These rare one-off performances in Paris combined with the regular influx of news from other cities to keep the public aware of Farrenc's symphonic works and of their conspicuous absence from the programs of the city's major orchestra, the orchestra of the Société des Concerts du Conservatoire. In February 1851, a notice in the *Revue et Gazette musicale* voiced the editor's dismay:

We have heard, and we express on our behalf, the regret that the committee of this Society [des Concerts du Conservatoire] did not believe it necessary to grant the honors of performance to one of the symphonies composed by Farrenc: We would have seen it not only as an act of gallantry, but of justice. It is such a rare exception that a woman composes symphonies with real talent; she deserves to be encouraged, and the danger of overabundance is not to be feared.[10]

In his multi-part article on the state of modern music published in summer 1851, just a few months after the second public performance of the Nonet, the critic Edouard Fétis (the son of the historian, theorist, critic, and conductor François-Joseph Fétis) wrote about Farrenc's exceptional accomplishments and their importance as a sign of new social developments to come. In a section on the "rebirth of the symphony in France," Fétis notes the ingrained, structural biases that had long kept women from participating in public life and/or from receiving due recognition for their work and abilities, then he goes on to describe Farrenc's contributions to demonstrate women's potential as equal participants in the full range of classical styles and genres:

We have become accustomed to seeing women emerge from the sphere of inaction *where our prejudices had long maintained them*. We are no longer surprised that they distinguish themselves in various branches of the arts and even sciences that were once supposed to be inaccessible to them. However, there are still jobs for which their aptitude is not recognized. Thus, *we admit that a woman succeeds in miniature and in romance; but we do not suppose that she could produce a historical picture or a symphony.* Madame Farrenc has refuted this belief with regard to music. We will not say that the symphonies she composed are marked with the seal of genius; but it is enough that they demonstrate real knowledge; it is enough that the style is elegant and pure, that the orchestra is finally directed with a firm hand through the developments of a well-conceived plan, for there is reason there to extend congratulations justly to Madame Farrenc.[11]

In the subsequent installment, Fétis discusses chamber music in France and includes "Madame Farrenc, whose works have a serious merit which has nothing feminine about it" in a listing of composers who had "remained faithful to chamber music."[12] (The list also includes Ferdinand Hiller, August de Sayve, and Carl Schwencke.)

Despite the neglect of her orchestral works, Farrenc's chamber music was performed in salon matinées and evening concerts throughout the 1850s, to increasing acclaim. A performance "in the salons of Monsieur B." in December 1854 included Farrenc's first quintet for piano and strings played by her student Louise Salomon, and the review that followed indicates Parisian audiences's devotion to chamber music and to Farrenc's works in particular:

This remarkable composition was listened to with a religious attention, and the lively applause proved to the author and the executants the satisfaction of the audience, which included several artistic luminaries. Madame Farrenc is today, in the opinion of everyone, one of the glories of the French school in musical composition. One finds in her works a great merit of construction, original ideas that denote individuality, a gracious style, always elevated, and a great knowledge of the effect of instruments.[13]

The repeated performances of the Nonet that Farrenc, her students, and her colleagues facilitated in the 1850s and 1860s, and the frequent references in reviews to the Nonet as a sort of "symphony in miniature," served as a reminder that her musical talents extended beyond the piano and the chamber to include large-format music that only a few lucky listeners had so far had a chance to hear.

The success of the Nonet led Farrenc to compose additional works that surely would not have come to light without the stimulus of collaboration with specific musicians interested in her compositional style (i.e., wind players). Their advocacy for the Nonet and for her other works would lead to further performances and recognition for Farrenc and her music throughout the 1850s and 1860s. Louis Dorus (1812–1896) may have been a driving force in creating opportunities for the public to hear Farrenc's music. He played the flute part in all five documented performances of the Nonet as well as several performances of the Sextet for piano and wind quintet (flute, oboe, clarinet, bassoon, and horn) that Farrenc completed in 1852. Farrenc premiered the Sextet with members of the now defunct Society for Classical Music in a matinée at the home of Sophie Pierson-Bodin just after its composition, and she and her pupils played on several subsequent concerts with Dorus and others from the Nonet ensemble. Dorus and his family maintained close ties with Farrenc; the two frequently performed together and singly on each other's concerts, and Farrenc taught his daughter Juliette piano in her private studio. Farrenc dedicated her *20 Études of Medium Difficulty for Piano*, Op. 42, to Juliette, and she composed the *Trio for Piano, Flute, and Cello*, Op. 45, around 1855 for performance with Louis, to whom she dedicated the work when it was published years later. Farrenc honored the clarinetist Adolphe Leroy (1827–1880) in a similar way. He also participated in all of the documented performances of the Nonet and Sextet during Farrenc's lifetime, and her *Trio for Piano, Clarinet, and Cello*, Op. 44, was dedicated to Leroy when it was published in 1855–1856. Both of these works were published in alternate versions that substituted a violin for the wind instrument, a practical arrangement that made the works more marketable as standard piano trios. This small concession to the marketplace allowed those two works to circulate in Europe and (potentially) to be performed outside of Paris and made them more readily discoverable by later performers, while the Nonet and Sextet both remained unpublished until the late twentieth century. It is not clear why Farrenc chose to leave these works unpublished in her lifetime. All of her chamber music was self-published (or published by Aristide's firm), though the German firm Friedrich Hofmeister in Leipzig produced an edition of the two piano quintets. (These were Farrenc's only chamber works published outside of Paris in her lifetime.) Her countryman

George Onslow seems to have had no problem finding a publisher for his Nonet for Winds and Strings, Op. 77, around 1851 with the Parisian firm Brandus (the Hofmeister catalog of new publications lists the Leipzig firm Kistner as the publisher in 1851, which may indicate simultaneous editions) or for his earlier Sextet in E flat Major, Op. 30, for Piano, Flute, Clarinet, Bassoon, Horn, and Double Bass, with Breitkopf und Härtel in 1825. It is quite possible that the expense of having her larger-scaled works engraved deterred Farrenc from publishing them, given that it would have been difficult to recoup that cost with a work that required a specialist ensemble of so many players, compared to the piano trios and sonatas. (Onslow was independently wealthy, not a working musician, so the cost of the engraving likely would have been no deterrent, if he did have to bear the expense himself.)

By the end of the 1850s, with these four wind-focused works completed – and an additional sonata for piano and cello that she composed in 1857 and dedicated to Charles Lebouc – Madame Farrenc's collection of chamber music comprised a dozen works for an unusually varied collection of ensembles. At fifty-three years old, she was in the prime of her career and would surely have continued adding to this rich catalogue, if not for the tragedy of her daughter's death in January 1859 at the age of thirty-three. Victorine Farrenc was a talented pianist and composer; she studied with her mother at home and then at the Conservatory, where she won first prize in the annual piano class exercises in 1845 and 1846. In addition to playing her mother's works, she was known for her renditions of concertos by Hummel, Mozart, and Beethoven. She became ill with an unknown/unnamed disease around 1847, after which only two performances are documented, both in the Farrenc family's house concerts. According to her death certificate, she died at an Augustinian cloister in Versailles, where she likely was receiving hospice care.[14] Farrenc composed no new music after 1859, though she did resume performing and hosting concerts around 1861 to promote her collaborative work with Aristide on the *Trésor des Pianistes*, a collection of historical keyboard music, and she saw her completed works through the publication process in the 1860s.

The Prix Chartier

Although it did not lead to local performances of her orchestral music by Parisian ensembles, the Nonet and the new compositions and performances that it prompted in the decade following its premiere in 1850 helped to secure for Farrenc a measure of official recognition that eluded most women composers in the nineteenth century. In 1861, in recognition of her body of work, Farrenc was awarded the Prix Chartier, a newly endowed prize created to celebrate special achievements in chamber music and administered by the Academy of Fine Arts (Académie des Beaux Arts). This learned society grew out of the merger of three longstanding academies that had been established in the seventeenth century to administer and organize royal patronage of painting, music, and architecture. (Under the umbrella organization of the Insitut de France, they continue to manage the nation's many artistic institutions and national heritage sites, to sponsor public schools, and to award prizes and grants to meritorious artists and scholars into the present day.) The Academy of Fine Arts did not admit women members until the twentieth century, and their most prestigious prize, the Grand Prix de Rome, which provided a stipend and lodging for French artists and composers to study and work in Rome for three to five years with no further obligations, was not awarded to a woman until the twentieth century. (Lili Boulanger became the first woman to win the Prix de Rome in 1913; her older sister Nadia, who would go on to train many of the twentieth century's most important and iconic composers, gave up after four unsuccessful attempts.)

No official rules or regulations prevented women from holding a membership or competing for prizes, and in its earlier iterations the Academy of Painting and Sculpture had admitted women in the eighteenth century, including portraitist Elisabeth Vigée-Lebrun. But, as noted in earlier chapters in this volume, Farrenc and other women musicians in the nineteenth century were not considered for such awards and honors because they did not have the same access to public music spaces that men enjoyed – they could not be admitted to harmony and composition classes at the Conservatory, they could not (by tradition and social expectations of the day) conduct their own orchestral or choral works in public concerts, and they were largely excluded from the professional social networks that supported public musical careers. Instead, women musicians created and sustained a network of private and semi-private musical opportunities, in which chamber music became the most important way to demonstrate compositional and performative learning and finesse.

The Prix Chartier, then, provided a method to publicly celebrate and reward musical activities that took place (mostly) in private spaces. It was created in 1858 at the death of Parisian music lover Charles-Hyacinthe-Suzain-Jean Chartier, who left a substantial sum of money to the Academy via his estate in order to provide, "an annual annuity of 700 francs for the next 100 years, in recognition of the best works of chamber music, trios, quartets, etc. that will come closest to the masterpieces of this genre."[15] When the first prize became available in 1861, the music section of the Academy determined that it would be most in keeping with Chartier's wishes to, "go out and find excellence, rather than summon it to us ... to search out compositions inspired by a sincere love of the art, rather than to force into being a piece of work which might not always be indicative of a true calling," as reported by academy member Ambroise Thomas.[16] This process differed significantly from the academy's usual way of awarding musical prizes such as the Prix de Rome, which required applicants to compose a cantata or operatic scene based on a text provided by the committee, an academic exercise that had little to do with the applicant's prior experience or their musical interests and talents. The committee's decision to seek out worthy candidates for the Prix Chartier allowed them to focus on composers who had long been engaged in the art of chamber music and could demonstrate a clear record of meaningful contributions. The first prize was awarded in February 1861 to violinist Charles Dancla (1817–1907). A prolific composer of violin duos, piano trios, and string quartets, in addition to études and virtuoso showpieces, Dancla taught violin at the Paris Conservatory from 1855 to 1892. As noted in Chapter 1, he was impressed by Baillot's chamber concerts during his early years in Paris and formed a chamber ensemble with his younger siblings that gave regular concerts throughout the 1840s. (The brothers Charles, Arnaud Philippe, and Léopold made a living as professional string players; their sister Laure played, taught, and composed for the piano. All four studied at the Conservatory in the 1830s, taking first prize in their various areas of specialty.) In other words, like Louise Farrenc, Dancla had devoted considerable energy to chamber music as a composer, performer, and concert organizer.

Just seven months later, the committee was charged with selecting another awardee for the Prix Chartier. The 1861 notice published in *Le Journal des Savants* notes that "the Academy, having had two of these annuities at its disposal this year, awarded the prize to Mr. Charles Dancla on February 23 . . . . In its session on September 28, it awarded this prize to Madame Farrenc."[17] The details of this decision, though, merit some examination because they suggest the value of Farrenc's multi-faceted approach to her musical career, especially the importance of her salon performances. At the September meeting, the music section presented three candidates among whom they wanted to split the prize: Adolphe Blanc, Eugène Sauzay, and Louise Farrenc. Blanc and Sauzay were both well regarded violinists and leaders of chamber music groups, as well as composers of string quartets, piano trios, and other chamber works; they both taught at the Conservatory, and both had been considered as candidates for the prize in February. When this decision was presented to the full academy membership, though, the members held a vote and chose not to affirm the composers's choice, but rather to reject the idea of a shared prize and to award the full stipend to Madame Farrenc. The academy's decision to honor Farrenc alone suggests that her music and her reputation extended beyond the musical community of Paris to include artists, writers, and architects. Farrenc's ongoing engagement with a vibrant network of salonnières, performers, and former students who went on to become important patrons and salonnières themselves – not to mention the wives of influential businessmen and patrons in the Paris community – may have helped her to catch the attention of academy members, who likely participated in those salons and attended both public and private concerts like those hosted by the Farrenc family. This prestigious official recognition confirmed Farrenc's standing in

France's musical and artistic community. She wrote to the academy secretary, composer Fromental Halévy, to acknowledge receipt of his news and to say that she was "happy at having been singled out by judges whose approbation bestows the greatest honor upon me."[18]

The wind chamber works that Farrenc composed in the wake of the Nonet's success secured for her a second Prix Chartier in 1869. After noting that George Mathias and Eugene Sauzay were considered for the prize that year, and that they had both composed distinguished chamber music, the president's report notes,

The Academy's choice fell on Madame Farrenc, who has also continued to enrich with works of the greatest merit, the genre preferred by the donor [chamber music] and who had already obtained the prize in 1867 [sic, 1861]. The compositions published since then by this eminent artist shine with the purest classical style and elevated tendencies for which the Chartier Prize has contributed greatly to maintaining respect.[19]

The works published since 1861 were not new compositions, but works whose publication had been delayed until the later 1860s: the Trio for Piano, Clarinet, and Cello, Op. 44 (1854–1856, premiered 1856, published 1861); the Trio for Piano, Flute, and Cello, Op. 45 (1854–1856, premiered 1856, published 1863); and the Sonata for Piano and Cello, Op. 46 (composed and premiered 1857, published 1861). Guillaume does not disclose in his public report that the decision to award the prize to Farrenc followed the same procedures as the earlier deliberations: According to the meeting minutes for June 26, 1869, the musicians section proposed to split the prize among the three candidates (Mathias, Sauzay, and Farrenc), but the full session voted again not to divide the prize.[20]

The Posthumous Legacy of Farrenc and Her Nonet

After Farrenc's death in September 1875, the Nonet seems to have been largely forgotten along with the rest of her chamber music until its revival in the late twentieth century. However, several articles on the symphony in France include favorable discussions of Farrenc's work in that genre, including a 1923 assessment by

Georges Servières.[21] Farrenc's work on the *Trésor des Pianistes* was also recognized from time to time as an important contribution to the history of music. In the increasingly nationalist climate of the France's Third Republic, musicians pursued a distinctly French national heritage and musical style that would revitalize and modernize French musical society. An important institution founded with this aim in mind was the Société Nationale de Musique, whose motto was "Ars Gallica" (French Art). The Society's founders included Camille Saint-Saëns, César Franck, and Gabriele Fauré, who were described at the time as "serious, reflective" composers, "attracted less to the theater than to pure music."[22] As we have already seen, for most French musicians and writers about music in the nineteenth century, "serious" and "pure" music meant German or Viennese Classicism. Michael Strasser has demonstrated that at the time of its founding, the restorative agenda of the Society was less anti-German than it was anti-frivolity, a rebuke of what the members saw as the vapid or decadent spectacles of Second-Empire Paris and its apparent love of light musical entertainments, especially operetta. The Society at first was devoted to presenting young French composers' works in the context of "modern" Germanic examples (Wagner, Schumann, and Liszt) to introduce the French to modern compositional techniques and to promote their adoption by French composers. The works of earlier generations like Farrenc and George Onslow who had subtly adapted the Viennese Classical style to their local social and cultural context were cast aside or overlooked in favor of newer, more harmonically and formally daring music, such as the chamber music, piano pieces, and songs of César Franck, Camille Saint-Saëns, and Gabriel Fauré. Although polemicists and musicians disagreed as to the correct path forward for French music in this new climate, they generally agreed that instrumental music based in the Viennese Classical traditions was no longer relevant to a reformed French society seeking to reclaim a dominant position on the world stage after a humiliating defeat in the Franco-Prussian War of 1870–1871.[23]

Yet, in discussions of women composers and women's role in musical life during the late nineteenth and twentieth centuries, Farrenc's name continued to be associated with the best achievements of earlier generations. In the 1870s through the end of the century, some critics and musicians grappled with women's place in the professional world, and Farrenc's accomplishments inevitably were cited as examples of female excellence in an arena dominated by men. These discussions, though often maddeningly misogynistic when read today, at least demonstrate that Farrenc's reputation as a composer extended beyond continental Europe to both England and North America. For example, in 1877, the *National Journal of Education* based in Boston published an unsigned article addressing "the woman question" for teaching specifically. The author lists eight women professors from the eighteenth and nineteenth centuries, including Madame Farrenc and Loïsa Puget among the scientists Laura Bassi (1711–1778) and Mrs. (Mary) Somerville (1780–1872), the linguist and poet Clothilde Tambroni (1758–1817), and the painters Rosa Bonheur (1822–1899) and Elizabeth Thompson (1846–1933), before concluding: "But it would seem to require a wider induction than any known catalogue of such professional celebrities, to fix a general law for the whole sex."[24]

In case readers are tempted to characterize this 1877 assessment as a relic of a different cultural era, be reminded that at least as recently as 2015 the head music examiner for one of Britain's largest exam boards responded to a student email asking why no women were included among the sixty-three composers studied in its A-level music syllabus with the statement, "Given that female composers were not prominent in the western classical tradition (or others for that matter), there would be very few female composers that could be included."[25] (The Board adjusted the syllabus for the following year by adding works by five women: Clara Schumann, Rachel Portman, Kate Bush, Anoushka Shankar, and Kaija Saariaho.) This 2015 incident is ironic, given that over 100 years earlier, in 1883, the *Proceedings of the Royal Musical Association* had published a report from the English organist and music critic Stephen S. Stratton (1840–1906) on the accomplishments of women musicians despite the many impediments they faced through lack of access to education and professional opportunities dictated by social custom. On the education of women, for example, Stratton notes, "I think it will be conceded that, until quite recent times, the education of women was of a very meager character generally, and in some ranks of life could hardly be said to exist at all. In spite of this, many women of learning may be cited."[26] Among important female musicians, Stratton cites Louise Farrenc alongside Élisabeth Jacquet de La Guerre, Hélène de Montgeroult, Marie Bigot, Sophie Gail, Loïsa Puget, and Louise Bertin as figures already well known from Henry Chorley's book *Music and Manners in France and Germany* (vol. 1, 1841).[27] After responses from various members of the Association, the report concludes with a list of women composers, "compiled as evidence that women have been engaged in composition for a longer period of time, and in more branches of the art, than is generally supposed."[28] The seven-page list includes over 400 names with indications of the kinds of works each woman composed. Louise Farrenc's listing notes "Symphony, Overtures, Nonet, etc. etc."[29] Even this brief mention confirms the Nonet's centrality to Farrenc's reputation as a great composer in the decades following her death.

As these reports suggest, even among those who sought out the works of women composers and who knew of Farrenc's many accomplishments, the relative scarcity of performance opportunities, which reinforced broader society's seeming disbelief that a woman could write meaningful "serious" works (despite the evidence before them), and music culture's ever-onward progression that demands the new and innovative, meant that Farrenc's music fell out of favor around 1900. Near the end of the twentieth century, though, as the feminist movement prompted scholars to reclaim the lost or abandoned legacy of women artists and musicians, Farrenc took her place alongside Hildegard of Bingen, Marianne Martinez, Clara Schumann, and Fanny Hensel as a member of the nascent canon of women and underrepresented composers that emerged during this period of rediscovery.

Farrenc's music for winds and strings was at the forefront of this revival in new recordings, new published editions of her chamber music, and inclusion in important anthologies and textbooks about women musicians. The revival of Farrenc's music was made possible, in large part, because of the work of scholar Bea Friedland, whose book *Louise Farrenc (1804–1875): Composer,*

Performer, Scholar (1980, first published in 1975) has been cited throughout this study. Friedland's efforts represent the first scholarly assessment of Farrenc's music and the first investigation into her manuscripts and letters preserved at the national library of France in Paris (Bibliothèque nationale de France). As noted in Chapter 1, it remains the only available English-language book on Farrenc, despite some errors and omissions that beg correcting in an updated study.[30] Friedland's pioneering work, also disseminated in an article published in *Musical Quarterly* in 1974, brought Farrenc's music to the foreground and led to her inclusion in the first major (English-language) reference source for the study of women's music, the *Historical Anthology of Music by Women*, published in 1987.[31] This collection of score excerpts included the first movement (Allegro deciso) of Farrenc's Flute Trio, Op. 45, prefaced with a short introduction by Friedland. Similarly, the *New Grove Dictionary of Music and Musicians* published in 1980 as the first major overhaul of this august reference source included an entry on Farrenc by Friedland, as did the 1994 *New Grove Dictionary of Women Composers*.

The 1980s and 1990s saw the first recordings of works by Farrenc, including the Nonet. When violinist Marnie Hall produced a two-disc box set of LPs (long-playing records) titled "Women's Work" in 1975 on her record label Gemini Hall, she included the Scherzo from Farrenc's second Piano Quintet, Op. 31. This is probably the first commercial or professional sound recording of Farrenc's music. More followed shortly thereafter: A selection of piano works appeared on a record produced by the Musical Heritage Society in 1979, and the Nonet was recorded by the Bronx Arts Ensemble for Leonarda Productions in 1981. (Leonarda Productions was founded in 1979 "to promote contemporary music in general and historical music by women composers"; the Bronx Arts Ensemble included Marnie Hall on violin.[32]) The Finale of the Nonet from this recording and the Flute Trio's Scherzo were included in the compilation *Women Composers: The Lost Tradition Found* that accompanied the textbook of the same name by Diane Peacock Jezic in 1988. The 1990s also saw new publications of Farrenc's music in collections (such as Jeffrey Kallberg's ten-volume edition of *Piano Music of the*

Parisian Virtuosos from 1993[33]) and a series of thirteen editions published by the Pennsylvania-based feminist music press Hildegard Publishing Company, which issued an edition of Farrenc's own arrangement for string quintet (two violins, viola, cello, and double bass) of the Nonet in 2001.[34] The first modern edition of the Nonet was published by the British publisher Spartan Press in 1994, and another edition followed soon after in 1996 by the American-based firm International Opus.[35] Given these late dates, it is not clear from what edition the Bronx Arts Ensemble played in their 1981 recording; perhaps they had access to copies of the manuscript housed at the Bibliothèque nationale, or one of the members had made a set of parts from that source for their own use. Between 1998 and 2005, the German publisher Florian Noetzel issued a thirteen-volume critical edition of Farrenc's orchestral and chamber music, producing a new critical edition of the Nonet edited by Katharina Herwig in 2000 and used as the basis of the analyses and musical examples in this book.[36]

Further recordings and concert performances of Farrenc's works have continued throughout the early decades of the twenty-first century to rave reviews by critics. Reviewing a commercial release of the Nonet with several other works recorded at a live event at the Louvre in Paris in 2006, critic Elaine Fine noted, "The [American Record Guide] reviewers who have written about Louise Farrenc's music seem to agree that she was an excellent composer. Since I first heard her music I hoped that I would hear it performed and recorded often."[37] Just a few months later, she wrote in a review of Farrenc's Violin Sonata, Op. 39, "I am more impressed with Louise Farrenc (1804–75) every time I hear a new piece."[38] Six years later, Jerry Dubins began a campaign to bring greater attention and respect to Farrenc's works at *Fanfare* magazine through his laudatory reviews of new recordings of Farrenc's music. Some of these, ironically if perhaps not self-consciously, borrow some of the language used in Farrenc's own lifetime to make the case that the composer was the equal of any of her male colleagues. In 2009, for example, he wrote,

If any woman deserves to be recognized as the greatest female composer of the 19th century, it's Louise Farrenc. But I will go even a step further and say that during the period in which she was active as a composer – roughly the mid 1820s through the late 1850s – few composers of any gender persuasion, save for Felix Mendelssohn, could hold a candle to her when it came to writing symphonies and large chamber-ensemble works. . . .

No excuses or rationalizations need be made for the fact that she was a woman. Her music has more testosterone going for it than does the music of some biologically male composers.[39]

In 2018, Dubins could write, "I'm pleased to see that Louise Farrenc is coming to be seen more and more as a mainstream Romantic composer, able to hold her own alongside the big boys of the mid-19th century. . . . She is the real deal."[40]

Despite the relative lack of scholarly attention to Farrenc's music in recent years, the concert and recording industries have fully embraced her. Farrenc was featured as a "Composer of the Week" on the BBC 3 radio program hosted by Donald MacLeod in 2015, bringing greater public awareness to her works in the United Kingdom.[41] (The Manchester Music Festival planned to highlight Farrenc's works in 2020, but the festival was cancelled due to COVID-19 restrictions.) In 2021, a New York Times article by David Allen ("Louise Farrenc, 19th-Century Composer, Surges Back into Sound") likewise brought Farrenc to the attention of a new generation of American audiences.[42] Allen noted several recent and upcoming performances in the 2021–2022 season of Farrenc's music by major performance organizations, including the Philadelphia Orchestra and the Orchestre Métropolitain in Montreal (both under the leadership of conductor Yannick Nézet-Séguin), the National Symphony Orchestra, the Boston Handel and Haydn Society, and the Boston Chamber Players (featuring a November 2021 performance of the Nonet). His glowing assessment of Farrenc's music is peppered throughout with enthusiastic comments on its artistry and craftsmanship from the performers he interviewed, and it offered a fierce championing of the composer and her works that has been echoed since by writers for the Boston Globe (reviewing the Handel & Haydn Society performance), and the South Carolina Spoleto Festival, which included Farrenc's second Piano Quintet in its chamber music series in June 2022.

Since its rediscovery in the late twentieth century, the Nonet has become a centerpiece of Farrenc's oeuvre, with performances at major festivals and on important concert series becoming increasingly common. A work for a large chamber ensemble like this one has strong potential to anchor programs of miscellaneous ensembles. By surrounding the Nonet with a selection of duos, trios, or quartets for different subsets of instruments from the Nonet's instrumentation, concert organizers, recording producers and programmers, and university chamber music teachers can craft programs that celebrate the variety and spontaneity of making music among friends. In this way, the Nonet brings a bit of nineteenth-century salon conviviality back to life in the twenty-first-century concert hall.

Notes

1. "Mme Farrenc a du être heureuse du grand succès de cette soirée; il lui aura prouvé les sympathies du public pour des oeuvres sévères et pures que nous avons le regret d'entendre trop rarement." Thérèse Wartel, "Nonetto de Mme Farrenc" *Revue et Gazette musicale de Paris* 17/13 (March 31, 1850): 108.
2. Bea Friedland, *Louise Farrenc, 1804–1875: Composer, Performer, Scholar* (Ann Arbor: UMI Research Press, 1980): 42.
3. The program was advertised beforehand in "Nouvelles" *Revue et Gazette musicale de Paris* 18/12 (March 23, 1851): 94. Tickets cost six francs and could be obtained at the home of Madame Farrenc on the rue Taitbout.
4. "Les trois oeuvres qu'elle a fait entendre ont été extrêmement goûtées de tout l'auditoire." Adrien de La Fage, "Concert de Mme L. Farrenc" *Revue et Gazette musicale de Paris* 18/14 (April 6, 1851): 109.
5. "Revenons un instant à Mme Farrenc. Je ne parlerai pas de son exécution tout le monde sait qu'elle est irréprochable; mais n'y a-t-il pas lieu d'admirer tout autant le talent si solide et si sage qu'elle a su acquérir dans la composition? Le seul reproche à lui adresser, c'est d'être peut-être un peu trop sobre de ces heureuses hardiesses, de ces élans d'enthousiasme qui font pardonner à l'artiste jusqu'à des aberrations dans lesquelles la sûreté de goût de Mme Farrenc l'empêcherait certainement de se laisser entraîner. Le mérite dominant chez elle, c'est le naturel et la grâce; elle est de l'école de Haydn, mais elle a eu Hummel pour maître. Elle réussit merveilleusement dans le scherzo, et qui s'en étonnerait? Quelque sérieuse que soit une femme, elle aime toujours à badiner, et ce n'est pas moi qui lui reprocherai de badiner trop souvent. Une autre qualité du talent de

Mme Farrenc, c'est la juste proportion qu'elle sait donner au développement de ses pensées, de telle sorte qu'on n'ait jamais à lui adresser ce reproche auquel n'a pas même toujours échappé l'immortel Beethoven: C'est bien, mais c'est trop long.

Ajoutons que Mme Farrenc est presque la seule en France qui cultive encore la haute musique instrumentale, dont les compositeurs ne s'occupent plus. On a beau coup parlé de l'avenir, l'avenir de la femme pour la réforme de l'humanité; je me trouverais encore content si sa mission, pour continuer à parler le langage du jour, se bornait à ramener l'autre moitié du genre humain à la bonne musique, au bon goût et peut-être aussi au bon sens. Mais j'oublie que l'on dit chaque jour que nous possédons tout cela et au premier degré." Ibid.

6. "Que dire de cette œuvre? Que si Mme Farrenc n'avait pas déjà écrit d'excellentes symphonies, ce nonetto, symphonie au petit pied, la mettrait sur la voie, et ferait désirer aux nombreux partisans de son talent qu'elle se consacrât à ce beau genre de musique qui est le véritable drame lyrique, instrumental. Dans ce concert, qui était autant le sien que celui de la jeune cantatrice, la première des compositeurs féminins comme n'en possède aucun autre pays, s'est produite sous des aspects divers, et souvent d'une manière remarquable. Musique de chambre en style sévère et pur; dans des variations, pour un et plusieurs pianos, du genre à la mode; dans un air d'opéra italien, une *Didone*, où Mme Farrenc s'est fait justement applaudir, soit pour son talent d'écrire, soit dans la personne des excellentes pianistes qu'elle a formées par ses leçons." Henri Blanchard, "Concert de Mlle Valentine Bianchi." *Revue et Gazette musicale de Paris* 22/42 (October 21, 1855): 328.

7. "On savait qu'une réunion exceptionnelle d'artistes d'élite devait concourir à l'exécution d'une œuvre capitale, un nonetto … Ce morceau, admirablement interprété par MM. Sighicelli, Dorus, Barthélémy, Leroy, Rousselot, Villaufret, Casimir Ney, Alfred Marc et Gouffé, a effectivement électrisé l'auditoire. Plus on connaît les compositions de Mme Farrenc, plus on s'étonne que ses symphonies ne fassent pas partie du répertoire de nos concerts à grand orchestre; les vrais amateurs n'en mettent que plus d'empressement à saisir les occasions qui leur sont offertes d'entendre sa musique de chambre." "Nouvelles" *Revue et Gazette musicale de Paris* 32/53 (December 31, 1865): 430.

8. "Les variations de Fr. Schubert en quintette, exécutées par Mme Pierson, MM. Sighicelli, C. Ney, Marc et Gouffé, et le beau trio de Mozart par Mme Pierson, MM. Leroy et C. Ney, ont été entendus avec le plus grand plaisir. Des fragments d'une sonate de Beethoven pour piano seul, et un air varié pour le violon exécuté de la manière la

plus brillante par M. Sighicelli, ont complété ce riche programme." Ibid.

9. The concert and program were announced in "Nouvelles" *Revue et Gazette musicale de Paris* 13/16 (April 19, 1846), 127; Blanchard reviewed the concert in "Coup d'oil musical" *Revue et Gazette musicale de Paris* 13/19 (May 10, 1846): 147–148.

10. "Nous avons entendu exprimer, et nous exprimons pour notre compte le regret que le comité de cette Société n'ait pas cru devoir accorder les honneurs de l'exécution à l'une des symphonies composées par Mme Farrenc: on y aurait vu non-seulement un acte de galanterie, mais de justice. C'est une si rare exception qu'une femme qui compose des symphonies avec un vrai talent, qu'elle mérite d'être encouragée, et que le danger de la surabondance n'est pas à redouter." "Nouvelles" *Revue et Gazette musicale de Paris* 18/6 (February 9, 1851): 46.

11. "On s'est accoutumé à voir les femmes sortir de la sphère d'inaction *où le savaient longtemps maintenues nos préjugés.* On ne s'étonne plus qu'elles se distinguent dans diverses branches des arts et même des sciences qu'on supposait jadis ne leur être point accessibles. Cependant, il est toujours des travaux pour lesquels leur aptitude n'est pas reconnue. Ainsi, *l'on admet qu'une femme réussisse dans la miniature et dans la romance; mais on ne suppose pas qu'elle puisse faire un tableau d'histoire ou une symphonie.* Mme Farrenc adonné un démenti à cette croyance, en ce qui concerne la musique. Nous ne dirons pas que les symphonies qu'elle a composé es soient marquées du sceau du Genie; mais il suffit qu'elles accusent un savoir réel, il suffit que le style en soit élégant et pur, que l'orchestre y soit enfin dirigé d'une main ferme à travers les développements d'un plan bien conçu, pour fait qu'elle impressionne chaque qu'il y ait lieu d'adresser à Mme Farrenc de justes félicitations." Edouard Fétis, "Revue d'un Demi-Siècle. Musique Instrumentale" *Revue et Gazette musicale de Paris* 18/27 (July 6, 1851): 218, emphasis added.

12. "Parmi les compositeurs de musique de chambre, nous citerons … Mme Farrenc, dont les ouvrages ont un mérite sérieux qui n'a rien de féminin, nous en demandons pardon au beau sexe." *Revue et Gazette musicale de Paris* 18/30 (July 27, 1851): 242.

13. "Cette composition remarquable a été écoutée avec une religieuse attention, et de vifs applaudissements ont prouvé à l'auteur et aux exécutants la satisfaction du public, dans lequel se rencontraient plusieurs sommités artistiques. Mme Farrenc est aujourd'hui, de l'avis de tout le monde, une des gloires de l'école française dans la composition musicale. On trouve dans ses ouvrages un grand mérite de facture, des idées originales qui dénotent l'individualité, un style gracieux, toujours élevé, et une grande connaissance de l'effet des

instruments." *Revue et Gazette musicale de Paris* 21/52 (December 24, 1854): 416.

14. Heitmann, *Die Orchester- und Kammermusik von Louise Farrenc* (Wilhelmshaven: Florian Noetzel, 2002): 20.

15. "Nouvelles Littéraires. Institut Impérial de France. Académie des Beaux-Arts" *Le Journal des Savants* (October 1861), 649–653. www.gallica.bnf.fr (accessed 29 October 2023): 652.

16. Quoted in Friedland, *Louise Farrenc* (p. 52) from "Procès-verbal de la séance du 23 février 1861" (Paris, Archives de l'Académie des Beaux-Arts).

17. "Nouvelles Littéraires" *Le Journal des Savants* (October 1861) www.gallica.bnf.fr (accessed 29 October 2023): 652.

18. Friedland, 55.

19. "Rapport de M. [Claude?] Guillaume, Président de l'Académie des Beaux-Arts" *Academie des beaux-arts. Séance publique annuelle du samedi 18 décembre 1869* (Paris: Institut impérial de France, 1869): 14.

20. Friedland, *Louise Farrenc,* 55; citing the "Procès-verbal de la séance du 26 juin 1869" held at the Archives de l'Académie des Beaux-Arts in Paris. An online listing of winners for the years 1861 through 1942 suggests only one instance of a shared or split prize: August Morel and Charles Dancla, 1877. No comprehensive study of the Prix Chartier has been published, and (to my knowledge) no one has provided further insights into the archival records of the committee's deliberations in other years; it would be helpful to know how often and under what circumstances the committee proposed a prize-sharing option in later years.

21. Georges Servières, "La Symphonie en France au XIXe Siècle (avant 1870)" *Le Ménestrel* 85/41 (October 12, 1923): 413–416.

22. Romain Rolland, *Musiciens d'aujourd'hui* (Paris, 1908), quoted in Michael Strasser, "The Société Nationale and Its Adversaries: The Musical Politics of *L'invasion germanique* in the 1870s" *19th-Century Music* 24/3 (2001): 225.

23. Michael Strasser, "The Société Nationale and Its Adversaries"; and Brian Hart, "The Symphony and National Identity in Early Twentieth-Century France" in *French Music, Culture, and National Identity, 1870–1939,* ed. Barbara L. Kelly (Rochester, NY: Boydell & Brewer, 2008), 131–148.

24. The author also lists Lucrezia Conuors, about whom I can find no information. [Anon.], "A Broader Basis, and a Cooler Onset" *National Journal of Education* 5/18 (May 3, 1877): 210.

25. Nadia Khomami, "A-level music to include female composers after student's campaign" *The Guardian*, online edition (December 16, 2015) https://www.theguardian.com/education/2015/dec/16/a-

level-music-female-composers-students-campaign-jessy-mccabe-edexcel (accessed March 21, 2025).

26. Stephen S. Stratton, "Woman in Relation to Musical Art" *Proceedings of the Musical Association* 9 (1882–1883): 117.

27. Chorley describes Madame Farrenc as "of our own time, who also devotes herself to classical chamber-composition, and writes piano-forte quintettes, which are worthy, according to the critics, of honorable mention." Henry Chorley, *Music and Manners in France and Germany*, vol. 1 (London: Longman, Orme, Brown, Green, and Longmans, 1841): 11.

28. Stratton, 139.

29. Ibid., 142.

30. See also Heitmann, *Die Orchester- und Kammermusik von Louise Farrenc* and Catherine Legras, *Louise Farrenc, compositrice du XIXe siècle: Musique au féminin* (Paris: Harmattan, 2003).

31. James Briscoe (ed.), *Historical Anthology of Music by Women* (Bloomington: Indiana University Press, 1987).

32. [Anon.], "The Female Voice ... Now" *Institute for Studies in American Music Newsletter* X/2 (1981): 7. Leonarda Productions ceased operations in June 2019, according to the website archived at www.leonarda.com (accessed February 26, 2024).

33. Jeffrey Kallberg, *Native and Foreign Virtuosos: Selected Works of Zimmerman, Alkan, Franck, and Contemporaries. Piano Music of the Parisian Virtuosos, 1810–1860*, vol. 10 (New York: Garland, 1993). This edition includes Farrenc's *Rondeau* on a theme from Bellini's *Il Pirata*, Op. 9, and three Rondinos from the collection *Encouragement aux jeunes pianistes*, originally published in 1835–1836 without an opus number.

34. Louise Farrenc, *Quintet for 2 Violins, Viola, Cello, Bass: from the Nonet, op. 38*, ed. Susan Eileen Pickett (Bryn Mawr, PA: Hildegard, 2001).

35. Louise Farrenc, *Nonetto op. 38 for Flute, Oboe, Clarinet in B flat, Horn in E flat, Bassoon, Violin, Viola, Cello and Double Bass* (Kingussie, Scotland, UK: Spartan, 1994), no editor listed; and Farrenc, *Nonetto for Flute, Oboe, Clarinet, Bassoon, Horn, Violin, Viola, Violoncello and Double Bass, opus 38 (1849)* ed. William Scribner (Richmond, VA: International Opus, 1996).

36. Farrenc, *Nonett Es-Dur, op. 38*, ed. Katharina Herwig, *Kritische Ausgabe Orchester- und Kammermusik sowie ausgewählte Klavierwerke*, Teil II, Band 1 (Wilhelmshaven: Florian Noetzel, 2000).

37. Elaine Fine, "Review of *Farrenc: Nonet, Melody in B flat, ...* Naive 5033." *American Record Guide* 69/1 (January/February 2006): 114.

38. Elaine Fine, "Review of *Violin Sonatas by Women ...* Zuk 324" *American Record Guide* 69/5 (September/October 2006): 255.

39. Jerry Dubins, "Review of *Farrenc, Trio for Violin, Cello, and Piano, op. 33* … cpo 777 256" *Fanfare* 33/2 (November/December 2009): 160.
40. Jerry Dubins, "Review of *Farrenc Symphonies No. 2 and No. 3*" *Fanfare* 41/6 (July/August 2018): 184.
41. The episode is archived at www.bbc.co.uk/sounds/play/po376hgl (accessed February 26, 2024).
42. David Allen, "Louise Farrenc, 19th-Century Composer, Surges Back into Sound" *New York Times Online Edition* (October 8, 2021) www.nytimes.com/2021/10/08/arts/music/classical-music-farrenc.html; published in print edition of October 10, 2021, under the title "Her Bold Sounds Are Back in Style" (Section AR, p. 8).

BIBLIOGRAPHY

Nineteenth-Century Music Journals

Allgemeine Wiener Musik-Zeitung
Allgemeine musikalische Zeitung
La Revue et Gazette musicale de Paris
Le Journal des Savants
Le Ménestrel
Musikalisches Wochenblatt
Neue Zeitschrift für Musik
Revue musicale
Revue musicale, Journal des artistes, des amateurs et des théâtres

Secondary Literature

Abrams, Lynn. *The Making of Modern Woman: Europe, 1789–1918*. London: Routledge, 2002.

Allen, David. "Louise Farrenc, 19th-Century Composer, Surges Back into Sound." *New York Times Online Edition* (October 8, 2021) www.nytimes.com/2021/10/08/arts/music/classical-music-farrenc.html.

[Anon.]. "A Broader Basis, and a Cooler Onset." *National Journal of Education* 5/18 (1877): 210–211.

[Anon.]. "The Female Voice . . . Now." *Institute for Studies in American Music Newsletter* X/2 (1981): 7.

Bartlet, M. Elizabeth C. "A Newly Discovered Opera for Napoleon." *Acta Musicologica* 56/2 (1984): 266–296.

  "Grand Opera (Fr.)." *Oxford Music Online* https://doi.org/10.1093/gmo/9781561592630.article.11619.

  "Politics and the Fate of 'Roger et Olivier.' a Newly Recovered Opera by Grétry." *Journal of the American Musicological Society* 37/1 (1984): 98–138.

Briscoe, James (ed.). *Historical Anthology of Music by Women*. Bloomington: Indiana University Press, 1987.

Bibliography

Burnham, Scott. "A. B. Marx and the Gendering of Sonata Form." In *Music Theory in the Age of Romanticism*, 163–186. Edited by Ian Bent. Cambridge: Cambridge University Press, 1996.

Cadwallader, Allen and David Gagné. *Tonal Analysis: A Schenkerian Approach.* New York: Oxford University Press, 2007.

Caplin, William. *Classical Form: A Theory of Formal Functions for the Instrumental Music of Haydn, Mozart, and Beethoven.* New York: Oxford University Press, 1998.

Charlton, David (ed.). *Cambridge Companion to Grand Opera.* Cambridge: Cambridge University Press, 2003.

Chitty, Alexis, Maurice J. E. Brown, and Katharine Ellis. "Wartel Family." *Grove Music Online.* https://doi.org/10.1093/gmo/9781561592630.article.29929.

Chorley, Henry. *Music and Manners in France and Germany*, vol. 1. London: Longman, Orme, Brown, Green, and Longmans, 1841.

Citron, Marcia. *Gender and the Musical Canon.* Cambridge: Cambridge University Press, 1993.

Cypess, Rebecca. *Women and Musical Salons in the Enlightenment.* Chicago: University of Chicago Press, 2022.

Darcy, Warren and James Hepokoski. *Elements of Sonata Theory: Norms, Types, and Deformations in the Late-Eighteenth-Century Sonata.* Oxford: Oxford University Press, 2006.

Deaville, James. "Virtuosity and the Virtuoso." In *Aesthetics of Music: Musicological Perspectives*, 276– 296. Edited by Stephen Downes. Abingdon: Routledge, 2014.

Dubins, Jerry. "Review of *Farrenc, Trio for Violin, Cello, and Piano, op. 33* … cpo 777 256." *Fanfare* 33/2 (2009): 160.

"Review of Farrenc Symphonies No. 2 and No. 3." *Fanfare* 41/6 (2018): 184.

Ellis, Katharine. "Female Pianists and Their Male Critics in Nineteenth-Century Paris." *Journal of the American Musicological Society* 50/2–3 (1997): 353–385.

Music Criticism in Nineteenth-Century France: La Revue et Gazette musicale de Paris, 1834–1880. Cambridge: Cambridge University Press, 1995.

"The Limits of Seriousness: Piano Sonatas in 1840s Paris." In *Chopin's Musical Worlds: The 1840s*, 9–37. Edited by Artur Szklener. Warsaw: Narodowy Instytut Fryderyka Chopina, 2007.

"The Making of a Dictionary: François-Joseph Fétis, Aristide Farrenc, and the 'Biographie universelle des musiciens.'" *Revue belge de Musicologie* 62 (2008): 63–78.

Fauquet, Joël-Marie. *Les Sociétés de musique de chambre a paris de la restauration a 1870.* Paris: Amateurs de Livres, 1986.

"La Musique de chambre à Paris dans les années 1830." In *Music in Paris in the Eighteen-Thirties*, 251–298. Edited by Peter Bloom. Stuyvesant: Pendragon, 1987.

Fine, Elaine. "Review of *Farrenc: Nonet, Melody in B flat*, [...] Naive 5033."
   American Record Guide 69/1 (2006): 114.

   "Review of *Violin Sonatas By Women* [...] Zuk 324." *American Record Guide*
   69/5 (2006): 255.

Friedland, Bea. *Louise Farrenc, 1804–1875: Composer, Performer, Scholar*. Ann
   Arbor: UMI Press, 1980.

Gramit, David. *Cultivating Music: The Aspirations, Interests, and Limits of
   German Musical Culture, 1770–1848*. Berkeley: University of California
   Press, 2002.

Goldberg, Halina. "Chamber Arrangements of Chopin's Concert Works."
   Journal of Musicology 19/1 (2002): 39–84.

Goldberg, Halina. *Music in Chopin's Warsaw*. Oxford: Oxford University Press,
   2008.

Guillaume, Jean-Baptiste Claude Eugène. "Rapport de M. Guillaume, Président
   de l'Académie des Beaux-Arts." Academie des beaux-arts. Séance publique
   annuelle du samedi 18 décembre 1869. Paris: Institut impérial de France,
   1869.

Hart, Brian. "The Symphony and National Identity in Early Twentieth-Century
   France." In *French Music, Culture, and National Identity, 1870–1939*,
   131–148. Edited by Barbara L. Kelly. Rochester, NY: Boydell & Brewer, 2008.

Hascher, Xavier. "Schubert's Reception in France: A Chronology (1828–1928)."
   In *The Cambridge Companion to Schubert*, 263–269. Edited by Christopher
   H. Gibbs. Cambridge: Cambridge University Press, 1997.

Hepokoski, James. *A Sonata Theory Handbook*. Oxford: Oxford University
   Press, 2021.

Heitmann, Christin. *Die Orchester- und Kammermusik von Louise Farrenc*.
   Wilhelmshaven: Florian Noetzel, 2004.

   Louise Farrenc: Thematisch-bibliographisches Werkverzeichnis. Wilhelmshaven:
   Florian Noetzel, 2005.

Heitmann, Christin and Rebecca Grotjahn (eds.). *Louise Farrenc und die Klassik-
   Rezeption in Frankreich*. Oldenburg: BIS, Universität Oldenburg, 2006.

Hoyt, Peter A. "The Concept of *développment* in the Early Nineteenth Century."
   In *Music Theory in the Age of Romanticism*, 141–162. Edited by Ian Bent.
   Cambridge: Cambridge University Press, 1996.

Hyland, Anne. *Schubert's String Quartets: The Teleology of Lyric Form*.
   Cambridge: Cambridge University Press, 2023.

Joachim, Joseph. *Letters from and to Joseph Joachim, Selected and Translated by
   Nora Bickley*. New York: Vienna House, 1972.

Jullien, Adolphe (?). "Farrenc, Jeanne-Louise." In *Biographie universelle des
   musiciens et bibliographie générale de la musique*, 2nd ed., vol. 4, 186–188.
   Edited by François-Joseph Fétis. Paris: Didot Frères, 1866.

Kallberg, Jeffrey (ed.). *Native and Foreign Virtuosos: Selected Works of
   Zimmerman, Alkan, Franck, and Contemporaries*. Piano Music of the
   Parisian Virtuosos, 1810–1860, vol. 10. New York: Garland, 1993.

Bibliography

Keefe, Simon P. "Antoine Reicha's 'Dialogue': The Emergence of a Theoretical Concept" *Acta Musicologica* 72/1 (2000): 43–62.

Khomami, Nadia. "A-Level Music to Include Female Composers after Student's Campaign." *The Guardian*, online edition (16 December 2015) www.the guardian.com/education/2015/dec/16/a-level-music-female-composers-stu dents-campaign-jessy-mccabe-edexcel.

Kramer, Ursula. "Spohr und die Folgen: Eine kleine Geschichte des Nonetts." In *Kammermusik in "gemischten" Besetzungen: Christoph-Hellmut Mahling zum 70. Geburtstag*, 15–47. Edited by Kristina Pfarr and Karl Böhmer. Mainz: Villa Musica, 2002.

Kraus, Beate Angelika. "Elly Ney und Thérèse Wartel: Beethoven-Interpretation durch Pianistinnen – eine Selbstverständlichkeit?" In *Der "männliche" und der "weibliche" Beethoven, Bericht über den Internationalen musikwis-senschaftlichen Kongress vom 21. Oktober bis 4. November 2001*, 429–447. Edited by Cornelia Bartsch, Beatrix Borchard, and Rainer Cadenbach. Bonn: Beethoven-Haus, 2003.

Launay, Florence. *Les compositrices en France au XIXe siècle*. Paris: Fayard, 2006.

Legras, Catherine. *Louise Farrenc: Composatrice de XIXe siècle: Musique au féminin*. Paris: L'Harmattan, 2003.

"Les trios avec piano de Louise Farrenc." In *Le trio avec piano: Histoire, langages, et perspectives*, 73–92. Edited by Gérard Streletski. Lyon: Symétrie, 2005.

Leistra-Jones, Karen. "Staging Authenticity: Joachim, Brahms and the Politics of Werktreue Performance" *Journal of the American Musicological Society* 66/2 (2013): 397–436.

"(Re-)Enchanting Performance: Joachim and the Spirit of Beethoven." In *The Creative Worlds of Joseph Joachim*, 86–103. Edited by Valerie W. Goertzen and Robert W. Eshbach. Woodbridge: Boydell and Brewer, 2021.

Levin, Alicia. "'A Musician of the First Order': Frédéric Kalkbrenner's Virtuoso Strategies for Paris." In *Piano Culture in Nineteenth-Century Paris, 137–150*. Edited by Massimiliano Sala. Turnhout: Brepols, 2015.

Liszt, Franz. *Letters of Franz Liszt, Collected and Edited by La Mara*. Translated by Constance Bache. New York: Haskell House, 1968.

Locke, Ralph. "Paris: Centre of Intellectual Fervor." In *The Early Romantic Era: Between Revolutions: 1789 and 1848*. Edited by Alexander Ringer. Englewood Cliffs: Prentice Hall, 1991.

Ludwig, Alexander Raymond. "Expecting the Unexpected: Haydn's Three-Part Expositions." *Lumen* 32 (2013): 31–40.

Marx, Adolf Bernhard. *Musical Form in the Age of Beethoven: Selected Writings on Theory and Method*. Edited and translated by Scott Burnham. Cambridge: Cambridge University Press, 1997.

McClary, Susan. *Feminine Endings: Music, Gender, and Sexuality*. Minneapolis: University of Minnesota Press, 1991; revised second edition, 2002.

Bibliography

O'Hara, William. "The Composer as Master of All Developments." In *Antoine Reicha and the Making of the Nineteenth-Century Composer*, 115–152. Edited by Fabio Morabito and Louise Bernard de Raymond. Bologna: Orpheus, 2021.

Powers, Harold S. "'La Solita forma' and 'The Uses of Convention.'" *Acta Musicologica* 59/1 (1987): 65–90.

Ramaut, Alban. "Antoine Reicha et le Concept de Virtuosité: Approche Étymologique d'un Mot à la Frontière de deux siècles." In *Piano Culture in Nineteenth-Century Paris*, 115–136. Edited by Massimiliano Sala. Turnhout: Brepols, 2015.

Ratner, Leonard. *Classic Music: Expression, Form, and Style*. New York: Schirmer, 1980.

Reicha, Antoine. *Traité de Mélodie, Abstraction faite de ses rapports ave l'harmonie*. Paris: l'Auteur, 1814.

Traité de haute composition musicale. Paris: Zetter, 1826.

Rosen, Charles. *Sonata Forms*. New York: Norton, 1980.

The Classical Style: Haydn, Mozart, Beethoven. Expanded second edition. New York: Norton, 1997.

Schachter, Carl. *Unfoldings: Essays in Schenkerian Theory and Analysis*. New York: Oxford University Press 1999.

Schmalfeldt, Janet. *In the Process of Becoming*. Oxford: Oxford University Press, 2010.

Sowerwine, Charles. "Woman's Brain, Man's Brain: Feminism and Anthropology in Late Nineteenth-Century France" *Women's History Review* 12/2 (2003): 289–307.

Stefaniak, Alexander. *Schumann's Virtuosity: Criticism, Composition, and Performance in Nineteenth-Century Germany*. Bloomington: Indiana University Press, 2016.

Strasser, Michael. "The Société Nationale and Its Adversaries: The Musical Politics of *L'invasion germanique* in the 1870s." *19th-Century Music* 24/3 (2001): 225–251.

Stratton, Stephen S. "Woman in Relation to Musical Art." *Proceedings of the Musical Association* 9 (1882–1883): 115–146.

Sumner Lott, Marie. "Negotiation Tactics in Louise Farrenc's Piano Quintets, opp. 30 and 31 (1839–1840)." *Ad Parnassum* 8/15 (2010): 7–66.

The Social Worlds of Nineteenth-Century Chamber Music. Urbana: University of Illinois Press, 2015.

Talbot, Michael. *The Finale in Western Instrumental Music*. New York: Oxford University Press, 2001.

Tovey, Donald Francis. *Essays in Musical Analysis*, 6 vols. London: Oxford University Press, 1935–1939.

"Haydn's Chamber Music" in *The Mainstream of Music and Other Essays*, 1–64. London: Oxford University Press, 1949.

Uhde, Katharina. "Joachim and Brahms in the Spring and Summer of 1853: Formative Influences and Performative Identities Reconsidered." In *Rethinking Brahms,* 156–176. Edited by Nicole Grimes and Reuben Phillips. Oxford: Oxford University Press, 2022.

Vande Moortele, Steven. "In Search of Romantic Form." *Music Analysis* 32/3 (2013): 404–431.

"Romantic Forms." In *The Cambridge Companion to Music and Romanticism,* 258–276. Edited by Benedict Taylor. Cambridge: Cambridge University Press, 2021.

Wartel, Thérèse. *Leçons Écrites sur les sonates pour piano seul de L. van Beethoven.* Paris: Girod, 1865.

Watkins, Holly. *Metaphors of Depth in German Musical Thought: From E. T. A. Hoffmann to Arnold Schoenberg.* Cambridge: Cambridge University Press, 2011.

Webster, James. "Schubert's Sonata Form and Brahms's First Maturity." *19th-Century Music* 2/1 (1978): 18–35.

Wulfhorst, Martin. "Pierre Baillot: Against the Odds." *The Strad* 133/1582 (2022): 38–45.

INDEX

Alard, Jean-Delphin, 19, 30, 31, 35, 120

Baillot, Pierre, 17, 30–31, 43, 79, 128
Beethoven, Ludwig van, 11, 16, 94
    Quintet for Piano and Winds, Op. 16, 27
    Septet for Winds and Strings, Op. 20, 82,
        86, 88
Blahetka, Leopoldine, 8

Chartier, Charles-Hyacinthe-Suzain-
    Jean, 128
Cossmann, Bernhard, 37, 38–39, 40

Dancla, Charles, 30, 128, 129
de Malleville, Charlotte, 26, 33, 34
Dorus, Louis, 27, 43, 44, 47, 118, 120, 125

Farrenc, Aristide, 6, 7, 8, 9, 12, 42, 44, 47,
    58, 121, 123, 125, 126
Farrenc, Louise
  as performer, 8, 9–10
  as symphonist, 122–123, 130
  as teacher, 18–19, 132
  biographical sources, 4, 5
  Conservatory wage discrepancy, 19
  dedications, 8, 41
  network, 129
  works
    20 Études de Moyenne difficulté, Op.
      42, 125
    30 Études dans tous les tons majeurs
      et mineurs, Op. 26, 8, 13–14, 40
    Air russe varié, Op. 17, 12, 13
    early variation sets, 7
    Hymn russe varié, Op. 27, 40
    piano quintets, 18, 40, 95, 125
    Quintet for piano and strings, Op. 30,
      14, 44, 120, 124
    Quintet for piano and strings, Op. 31,
      14, 19, 41, 134, 136

Sextet for piano and winds, Op. 40,
    14, 125
Sonata for cello and piano, Op. 46, 14,
    126, 130
Sonata for violin and piano, Op.
    37, 14
Sonata for violin and piano, Op. 39,
    14, 120, 135
symphonies, 14, 18, 119, 122
Trio for clarinet, cello, and piano, Op.
    44, 14, 125, 130
Trio for flute, cello, and piano, Op. 45,
    14, 125, 130, 134
Trio for piano, violin, and cello, Op.
    33, 14
Trio for piano, violin, and cello, Op.
    34, 14, 41, 82
Variations brillantes on a theme by
    Aristide Farrenc, Op. 2, 7
Variations brillantes sur la cavatine
    d'Anna Bolena de Donizetti, Op. 15, 8
Variations on a theme by Count
    Wallenburg, Op. 25, 121
Variations on a theme of Bellini for
    three pianos, Op. 29, 120, 121
Variations on themes from Bellini's
    I Capuletti for piano duo, Op. 29, 18
Variations sur une galopade favorite
    hongroise, Op. 12, 8
Farrenc, Victorine, 11, 24, 41, 126
Form Function Theory, 65–66
Franchomme, Auguste, 19, 31, 120

Gouffé, Achille, 27, 43, 44, 47, 120

Hummel, Johann Nepomuk, 5–6, 9, 10, 11,
    24, 27, 30, 33, 39, 43, 47, 65, 93,
    120, 126
  Septet for Piano, Winds, and Strings, Op.
      74, 82, 88, 90–92, 95, 97

Index

Hummel, Johann Nepomuk (cont.)
  Septuor militaire for Piano, Winds, and
    Strings, Op. 114, 44

Joachim, Joseph, 25, 26, 27, 28, 36, 37, 39,
    40, 41, 47, 79, 118
  attitude towards Paris, 49
  performance of Bach's Chaconne, 119
juste milieu, 2, 13, 16–17, 22

Lebouc, Charles, 25, 27, 46, 121, 126

Marx, Adolf Bernhard, 64, 65
Mendelssohn, Felix, 14, 37, 39, 47, 93,
    114, 136
  performances of his music in Paris,
    38, 41
  Scherzos as models, 95

Ney, Casimir, 43, 47, 87, 120
Nézet-Séguin, Yannick, 136

Onslow, George, 1, 32, 43, 44, 65,
    93, 126
  Nonet for Winds and Strings, Op. 77, 43,
    44, 82, 87, 95
  Sextet for Piano, Winds, and Strings, Op.
    30, 126

Pierson-Bodin, Sophie, 8, 33, 46, 122, 125
purple patch (harmonic feature), 72, 109–111

Reicha, Anton, 5, 27, 58, 60, 66, 71, 72, 77,
    78, 82, 104

grande coupe binaire, 60–65, 67, 100,
    107–108
Romanticism, 14, 16–16, 65
Rossini, Giachino, 6, 7, 48, 70, 110

Schubert, Franz, 14, 66, 67, 72, 94, 109, 114
  reception in Paris, 37, 67–69, 122
Schumann, Clara, 5, 11, 33, 132, 133
Schumann, Robert, 11, 12, 14, 17, 43,
    66, 114
Société de musique Classique, 2, 27, 32,
    42–46, 49, 50, 58, 59, 92, 120
Société nationale de musique, 131
Society for Classical Music, see Société de
    musique
Sonata form
  gendered views, 64
Sonata Theory, 60, 63, 64
Spohr, Louis, 1, 43
  Nonet for Winds and Strings, Op. 31, 44,
    82, 87, 95

Tilmant, Théophile, 67–69

Wartel, Thérèse, 26, 34, 38, 50
  as a "serious" pianist, 26, 35
  as organizer of Classical Music Society,
    42–43
  concerts with Joachim and Cossmann,
    25, 27, 40
  Germany tour, 36–37
  relationship with Louise Farrenc, 40–41
  review of Farrenc's Nonet, 25, 26, 119
women composers (historiography), 131–133

For EU product safety concerns, contact us at Calle de José Abascal, 56–1°,
28003 Madrid, Spain or eugpsr@cambridge.org.